PRAISE FOR Winning Leadership

"What a brilliant blend of the inside and the outside work great leadership requires! Winn, a two-time Olympian, clearly lays out a path to more effective leadership that focuses on developing the core inner skills that make people mental athletes and masters of their minds. Each of the seven chapters is filled with action steps, stories, and insight that can make the difference between carrying the baggage of the past, with its ineffective thinking and feeling, and facing the future with the ability to engender collaboration, greater success, and the fulfillment of connection with self deeply rooted in authenticity. It takes curiosity, awareness, and practice. Kudos to Sherry Winn on this masterpiece!"

Elizabeth Power, M.Ed.
Fulbright Specialist in Trauma Informed Care
Founder, The Trauma Informed Academy™
Adjunct instructor, Psychiatry, Georgetown University Medical Center

"I recently read Sherry Winn's book, Winning Leadership. This book is a must-read for leaders looking to reach their full potential. I wish I had read this when I was in the corporate world; it's an invaluable resource for leaders. Sherry takes readers on a journey of self-discovery and empowerment. Her inspiring message provides straightforward, actionable advice on becoming an authentic leader who attracts and retains high-performing teams. Her seven secrets will help you become a more confident, powerful leader. They will also help you build trust with your team and gain respect from your peers. I highly recommend this book to leaders looking to make a difference in their workplace."

Kim-Adele
Director and Council Member of Barclays, International Best-Selling Author and Keynote Speaker, CEO of Kim Adele Ltd

"*Winning Leadership, Sherry Winn reminds us that 'thoughts are things.' Creating a winning culture, rests on how leaders view and treat their teams, and Winn – an award-winning coach –has compiled a highly-readable guide based on her experiences and those of other successful leaders. Each chapter of this book is filled with inspiring words of wisdom, practical tips and winning takeaways. Your first step toward success is simple: invest in this book today!*"

Danny Brassell Ph.D.,
Internationally-acclaimed Speaker and
Author, Executive Speaking Coach and Founder of lazyreaders.com

"*Powerful. Real. Practical. Soulful. We are all a part of teams: family, work, community and many more. Sherry provides the habits, practices, skills, and wisdom that you can apply immediately to lead you and your team to improved positive results. This book is a must have for every leader. Her real-world stories and insights are guaranteed to provide everything you need for YOUR team to Winn!*"

Louie Sharp
US. Marine (retired), VP of Sound Enhances (retired), Sharp Auto Body
Business Owner, Founder/CEO of The Gifted Leader

"*When it comes to leadership, Sherry Winn is the real deal! This book is insightful and chocked full of real-world observations, guidance and ideas. There are many leadership books – this one should be read cover-to cover and kept close at hand for the many times you will reference it! If you're looking to improve and sharpen your leadership skills, attitudes and abilities AND build the best team possible - read this book. Then, go execute and be a WINNING Leader!*"

Phil Gafka, CBC
Author – *Hole-In-One Leadership,* Leadership for Enterprises and
Professionals (LEAP) Coaching

"*Sherry shares the seven secrets of how she became the leader of leaders. She reveals the refreshing concept that leadership is not about ego, but about putting your team first. She embraces that winning comes from creating a culture where people can speak without fear and collaboration is as equally important as competition. I highly recommend this book as Sherry leads us through her personal experiences, real life examples and actionable processes for you to become the winning leader that you were meant to be!*"

Gary Barnes - The Breakthrough Business Mastery Coach
Gary Barnes International

"*Winning Leadership: Seven Secrets to Being A Truly Powerful Leader is an essential reading for any leader who believes in being a lifelong learner. Timely, astute, and enriching, Sherry offers a perceptive and pragmatic tool kit for navigating the disruptions of building a championship team.*"

Linda I. McCabe, President and Founder of Optimal Level, Speaker, Author, Successful Business Owner, Podcast Series Host of Lightning Strikes, Practical Wisdom for Everyday Success

"*You will love this book from the first page until the last page, because each page offers value. Sherry teaches you how to be a better leader using insight from her past clients and personal stories. Explaining through an objective lens, she offers tools that can be used in multiple situations. Because this book is so inviting, I finished it quickly so that I could apply her coaching tips in my own life and coaching practice.*"

Lindsay Mcdonnell, Author of DANCING WITH CANCER AND HOW I LEARNED TO LEAD: A guide to becoming an advocate for personalized cancer care, Speaker and Cancer Care Coach

"Sherry Winn has taken her experiences as an Olympian athlete and a collegiate coach, coupled with extensive research, to bring us proven winning formulas to lead and create teams that work exceptionally well together. This book is filled with brilliant insights and practical steps, concepts and questions to guide you to lead a team that can come together and perform at the highest level."

Amy Riley
The Courage of a Leader
Keynote speaker, #1 international best-selling author,
Leadership development consultant

Winning Leadership
Seven Secrets to Being
a Truly Powerful Leader

Finding and Keeping the Best People
While Building a Loyal Team of Champions

Sherry Winn

Winning Leadership
Seven Secrets to Being a Truly Powerful Leader
Copyright ©2023 UcanCreateSuccess LLC

ISBN 978-1506-911-52-6 AMZ
ISBN 978-1506-911-06-9 PBK
ISBN 978-1506-911-07-6 EBK

LCCN 2023TBD

April 2022

Published and Distributed by
First Edition Design Publishing, Inc.
P.O. Box 17646, Sarasota, FL 34276-3217
www.firsteditiondesignpublishing.com

Disclaimer: This book is designed to provide information and motivation to our readers; therefore, the advice and strategies herein may not be suitable for every situation. It is sold with the understanding that the Author and the Publisher are not engaged in rendering legal, psychological, or other professional services. Neither the Author nor the Publisher shall be liable for any physical, psychological, emotional, financial, or commercial damages, including, but not limited to, special, incidental, consequential, or other damages. You are responsible for your own choices, actions, and results. The fact that an organization or a website is referred to in this work as a citation or a potential source of further information does not mean that the Author or the Publisher endorses the information that the organization or website may provide or recommendations it may make. Further, the readers should be aware that internet websites listed in this work may have changed or disappeared between when the work was written and when it is read.

To all those leaders who took time to share their wisdom, vulnerability, and best secrets for creating winning cultures. They are givers, not takers. Men and women who took on the leadership role for more than the title and the salary. They became leaders, because they knew they could make a positive impact with their team members and organizations. All their names, titles, and organizations are shared in the acknowledgments.

A special thank you to Sarah Victory, Andree Martin, and my three constant companions who slept by my feet, required me to take breaks outside with them, and let me know that I was always adored: Piper, Aspen, and Sawyer.

Foreword

Leadership is the most misunderstood word in business.

Not sure this is true? Consider this...

You've probably read a few leadership books; where do they agree and where do they disagree? You've probably found more disagreement than agreement.

Do your own research: ask 10 people to define leadership and you'll probably get ten very different answers.

With this uncertainty, what's a leader to do?

You hold in your hands a book that can help you sort all of this out. You'll get a new perspective from Sherry Winn, a leader who has been lead and has led many different teams, through many different circumstances, with many different approaches, with different levels of success and failure. You get to learn from all of them.

Anyone can lead in good times.
It's the bad times that reveals a leader's true ability.

This isn't just one person's experience, self-lauding their wins, but a collection of perspectives, insights, winning moments, losing moments; all the scars and bruises from a lifetime of being lead and leading.

And it all leads to one solid conclusion: in leadership, **who** you are is way more important than **how** you lead.

Your relationship with yourself and your team members determines how you'll successfully lead them on the journey to the agreed destination. Without knowing and respecting their skills, motivations, aspirations, and fears, you'll blindly lead a horrific journey that no one wants to take.

The beauty of this book: it doesn't demand that you follow one specific leadership style, much like books authored by famous, celebrity leaders. Why? Because your leadership circumstance will probably never match theirs for which they are famous, such as running a billion-dollar company, leading soldiers into battle, or a launching a Wall Street darling unicorn. Do what they did and it's likely that you'll fail spectacularly.

There is no one path to leadership. But there are a few key principles.

Instead, you'll gain insights from 200 leaders who are much more like you, so that you gain a broad perspective of applicable leadership principles and concepts that match your situation.

With the insights you'll gather, you can work on who you are with a clear understanding of why that's essential, and what's important for you to be considering right now.

Along the way, you'll be educated and entertained by Sherry Winn's humility, authenticity, and full presence to key leadership principles.

This unique book on leadership will bring you a new, broad perspective on what to do, when to do it, and how to get it done, without getting mired in the ego of the author. What a relief!

You've read this far, now take the most important step... the next one... read the book with pen in hand making these wise ideas your own.

Mark S A Smith,
Business Growth Strategist
NimbilityWorks.com
Delivering executive development services author of too many business and leadership books to mention

The Winning Ways of Winning Teams

Everybody wants to play on a winning team, but very few people understand what it takes to be on a winning team.

As a youngster I thought all it took to be on a winning team was hard work. It was a simplistic view of teamwork, and one that didn't work very well for me. What I failed to understand was that *winning is defined by as much as who you are and how you show up as by how hard you work.*

It turned out that my teammates didn't want to play with me, because I brought too many emotional challenges with me— behaviors that failed to feed the emotional needs of a winning team. It took me years to figure out that winning teams were made up of people who valued others, spoke to them with respect, inquired about their needs, and took real interest in their lives.

As leaders, it is our responsibility to build a group of people with varying interests into a team of people who work well together and who spend less time in drama, gossiping, venting, complaining, misinterpreting, and tattling and more time resolving challenges that meet goals.

In the book, *No Ego: How Leaders Can Cut the Cost of Workplace Drama, End Entitlement, and Drive Big Results,* Cy Wakeman revealed that leaders spend about 2.5 hours per day dealing with the emotional waste of their team members. Imagine how those numbers play out: 2.5 hours x 5 days = 12.5 hours per week, 50 hours a month, and 600 hours a year. OUCH!

Those numbers reflect a single team within an organization. Imagine multiple departments with numerous team members. The number of hours dealing with problematic behaviors would be staggering. An organization of 1,000 employees with 20 leaders would yield approximately 2,400 hours of nonproductive work a year—that is 100 workdays!

I wish that I could tell you that I had discovered the secrets that I am going to share with you in this book before I became an Olympian in 1984 and 1988. The truth is that I hadn't yet found the winning formula of a leader. I knew the formula to become an Olympian and a starter, but not how to build a winning team.

During those years of training for the Olympics, I knew the team was missing something, and I blamed the coaches, because we spent more time cursing, yelling, finger pointing, mad, upset, and frustrated with one another than we did improving our skills. We said more "F yous" on the court than "Thank yous."

Since I knew firsthand from experience what didn't work, I set about learning what it took to be a winning leader. I read hundreds of books, observed people, recorded those reflections in my journal for 16 years, and discussed concepts with anybody who would take the time to share with me. What I learned was that people are complex beings and those complexities can either ignite or ruin good organizations quickly.

What we often do within our organizations is put band-aids on the gaping wounds of toxic behaviors and hope that the band-aids stick long enough for us to win the next sale, complete a project, or double our bottom line. We all want the same results—increased engagement, boosted productivity, enhanced innovation, and improved retention for better services and products. The way we get there is the journey that the book will take you through.

After retiring from the USA National Team, I embarked on 23 years of coaching collegiate athletics where I quickly learned that to win, we needed to overcome the learned belief systems that parlayed into losing mentalities. We needed to teach players how to self-manage so that conflicts were resolved quickly, constructive feedback was welcomed, responsibility was owned, communication was essential, and destructive behaviors were minimized.

The years that we emphasized teaching positive behaviors are the ones where we won championships, and the years where we failed to focus on building our people are the ones where we struggled to produce a winning season.

If we begin with the theory that everybody is skilled, smart, and possessed the capacity to learn, then through teaching, mentoring, and gentle questioning, we can guide them to recognize the behaviors that bring them success or cause them failure. We can change the fabric of our culture, the lives of our team members, and experience unprecedented success.

FROM DARKNESS TO THE OLYMPIC FLAME

Before embarking on the journey of this book which will give you the abilities to become an Olympic-level leader, it might be helpful for you to grasp me, the author of these words so that you can understand that all of us have a journey to get to where we want to be.

Imagine being born into the world with the announcement: Announcing a new member to the Winn starting lineup:

Game Day: 9/1/61
Hometown: Balmorhea, TX
Height: 18 inches
Weight: 6 lbs. 8 ounces
Position: **Star**

I grew into my starring role as a young athlete playing flag football and basketball with the boys during recess and beating most of them. I was quick, but mostly I had what coaches called moxie, the ability to understand the game and find a way to win.

In high school, I was an all-state athlete in three sports— volleyball, basketball, and softball. I was a straight "A" student and such a good girl that I got extra presents from Santa. I was an All-American Girl, the Golden Child, and Supergirl on the basketball court, and what I desired more than anything was to receive acknowledgement from my teammates, coaches, parents, and friends. What I got was a different story.

I grew up dreaming about being a good daughter, a valedictorian, and an Olympian. At the age of seven, when I witnessed my parents watching the Olympics in front of our black and white television, I knew that I wanted to become the very thing that they honored. I began working out in the mornings at 7:00 a.m. watching and imitating Jack LaLane, the first television fitness guru. I soon became a push-up, sit-up, and jumping jack queen.

As I grew older, my desire pushed me to the gym before school started, late in the evenings, and even traveling to the inner city of Fort Worth in a sweaty gym with no air conditioner to workout with the teenage boys and young men who gathered there. Not only was I the only girl in the gym, but I was also the only white person in the gym. Had my mother known where I was training, I might not have survived my youth.

Most people would think I was living the dream, training all the time, scoring at will against opponents on the basketball court averaging 28 points a game, but things never quite lived up to the stories created in other people's minds. My well-earned talents created jealousy and vengeance against me.

Imagine two starters quitting on the volleyball team because you are named captain or your teammates booing you when you were named MVP of a basketball tournament. Imagine a crowd full of people at a softball game cheering against you, yelling cruel chants and being so vicious that a policeman had to escort you to your car.

The more skills I gained, the more I found myself isolated. The more isolated I became, the more I wondered what was wrong with me. When I turned to my father and mother, they tried to comfort me, but they were in their own crisis—going through a blame-filled divorce.

When I went to college and discovered that the only friend I had was gay, I turned to the church elders for answers. The elders told me to drop the sinner, never talk to her again, and keep myself isolated from people like her. I didn't understand how the nicest and kindest person I knew should be shunned. Confused and angry, I drank to drown my sorrows.

My first college basketball game was at UCLA where the crowd chanted, "There is only two things from Texas, steers and queers, and we don't see any horns on you." I wondered, since I was hated by so many, if I could be gay.

Drinking was my self-medication. Drink and I could forget. Drink and I could be somebody different. Drink and my self-hatred would go away.

I didn't do well my first year in college struggling with drinking, questions about religion, sexuality, and the purpose of life. I felt like the world was against me. The less playing time I got, the more the cycle of self-hatred continued. That summer I went home to collect myself, to gain confidence, and to lose the twelve-pack around my waist that I had gained drinking booze.

My summer was filled with parents who were too fraught with their own pain to see mine. Lonely, I turned back to my passion—training. After working an eight-hour day, I lifted weights for an hour, ran three miles, and then shot 600 shots in the gym before crashing at night. During those hours of training, I was free, dreaming of playing in world-class venues and marching into the Olympic Stadium.

When I returned to college, I was ready to be the star I was born to be, certain that my path to adoration for my talents was soon to come. My sophomore year, I led the team in scoring and assists, yet once again I found herself among teammates who disliked me. I drank to drown the demeaning voices that crowded my mind in self-defeating talk.

My teammates complained to the coach that they couldn't play with me—that I was too different and too difficult to play with. My coach told me, "You are the best player that I have ever coached, and you could be All-American, but I can't let you be on a team if you cannot get along with your teammates."

My coach took me to the locker room and told the team to tell me what they thought about me. There were no rules around the discussion—no let's focus on solutions rather than blame, or let's use "I" statements rather than "You did" statements. It was open fire on my fragile mental state.

I don't remember all the bashing I received, but I do remember this statement, "It doesn't matter if Sherry changes, I still won't like her, because she is just the type of person who is unlikeable."

People will tell you that words cannot wound you, but I am here to tell you that words can make you bleed and can cut you so deeply that the scars last a lifetime. It is not often a single wound that causes us to crash. It is the wounds stacked upon each other and the belief systems around those wounds that cause the crash.

When I left the locker room, my dream slaughtered, I drank for two weeks straight. I drank until I passed out and then upon awakening, drank again. Toward the end of the two-week drunk, I awoke in the middle of the night to go the bathroom and found my partner in bed with my best friend. I didn't say anything, I just turned and walked away. I figured I was already the walking dead and nothing else could hurt me.

The next morning, I didn't reach for a drink. As I sat on my bed, tears streaming down my face, beer cans and pizza boxes littered around the floor, I reached for my .38 snub-nosed special. I sat like that for an hour, my finger on the trigger, pulling the gun up to my chin, and then back to the bed. I searched for some reason to go on, for some hint of goodness, but it seemed like my dreams were too far away. I couldn't imagine reaching the Olympics from where I sat...and yet, there was this image of me marching into the Opening Ceremonies that was unwavering.

I figured that I had three options:

1. Pull the trigger and hope that my aim was true.

2. Keep living the same miserable existence.

3. Change.

I put the gun down, kicked the cans and boxes out of the way, found my t-shirt, shoes, and running shorts and began training again. I quit drinking, read dozens of personal development books, journaled, and found people who saw the good in me. *I learned **new belief** systems, discovered **what part** I played in my journey, **gave up being a victim**, and worked on the leading-edge me.*

I took up a new sport called team handball and found myself playing in the National Team Handball Tournament in New York City. The U.S. National Coach took an interest in me and invited me to join the National Team in New Jersey to train for the 1984 Olympics.

The team trained twice a day year around for 3½ years and just like that, I was marching into the 1984 Opening Ceremonies along people such as Carl Lewis, Mary Lou Retton, and Michael Jordan. I went on to become a Two-Time Olympian and a National Championship Coach.

People began asking me how I was able to coach successful teams, what it took to become an Olympian, and how they could create successful teams and leaders. The more that people asked, it became a natural evolution for me to speak and write about winning leadership and winning teams. I became a three-time bestselling author and have spoken for up to 14,000 people at a time at companies such as Adobe, Edward Jones, New York Life, and Hitachi.

I share this story because wherever you are, there is hope. I didn't lead a magical life as some people tend to believe. What I did was learn the tools that helped the challenges become easier. Life still offers challenges, and I have learned the most powerful tool of all—that I can view the challenges as adventures rather than pain.

My passion is to support other leaders on their journey so that they can become Olympic-level leaders who empower their team to be champions. That is why this book is essential for you and your team—so that you can empower yourself and others to be winners in life.

WINNING QUOTES

"On our team, it is nonnegotiable that everybody buys into the team goal; there are no individual goals."
Amanda Weeks-Geveden, SVP, Managing Director, US Bank

"The secret of leadership is that it is 100% about people. You must find the right people with the right values, because you cannot teach integrity, intelligence, or ambition."
Andrew Laudato, COO, The Vitamin Shoppe

"The best teams are the ones that develop diversity of thought with the ability to work together."
Carla Borsoi, Head of Business Operations, Felt

"The path to true fulfillment is to serve others first."
Clark Twiddy, President, Twiddy & Company

"Bring your team members into the process. Be quiet. Listen. Figure out where they are and what they know. Look for the nuggets of truth in what they are saying."
Chuck Tooley, President, Tooley Communications

"Politics always exist in a system, and you must believe in the power of the individual to make change, or nothing ever moves forward."
Claire Darley, VP, Digital Media Field Sales & WW Customer Support, Adobe

"All business problems are people problems. Focus on your people and your business will soar."
Danny Wyrwas, Owner, Absolute Fence, Elevate Leadership & Business Consulting

"Don't let anybody's negativity hold you back."
Jennifer L Lovett, President/CEO, Crystal Financial Insurance Services

CHAPTER ONE

The Winning Factor

THE KEY TO CREATING POSITIVE CULTURES

When the Athletic Director from the University of Minnesota-Morris hired me for my first head basketball coaching position, I called my father who was a former high school coach. I asked, "Dad, what offense should I run?"

He replied, "Honey, it doesn't matter."

"What do you mean it doesn't matter? This is my life, my dream, my career. Of course, it matters!"

"Honey, what matters is if you can get the team to run the offense together."

My father's wisdom worked well for me during the 23 years that I coached college basketball where my teams made it to the Elite Eight three times and won a National Championship. What was effective in those years that we won the big ones is that the team played well together. There were years where we had incredible talent but where players, despite wanting to win, allowed their subconscious biases influence how they played or didn't play with others.

Playing together sounds like such a simple concept, and it is. BUT, playing together is rarely simple.

In the corporate and nonprofit world, leaders categorize not playing well with others as silos where one department refuses to work with another department, or where one leader will not share information with other leaders. On the playground, this would be equivalent to taking the only ball and going home.

Playing together isn't easy because you can't tell people to leave their personal history at the door. You can't tell them to stop thinking a certain way that cancels a behavior which has served them well.

You can't tell people to forget about their divorce, the spouse who cheated on them, the looming bankruptcy, or their drinking, gambling, or drug problem. You cannot separate people from their life experiences. People define themselves through their life experiences.

In fact, we don't see life as it is; we see life as we are.

One of the biggest challenges for leaders is not what people think. It is not about producing an excellent product or service, which takes imagination and ingenuity. It is not about marketing, which is a hirable talent. It is not about venture capital or securing loans. Most business owners can achieve those first steps. One of the greatest challenges for leaders is to create and maintain a culture where people want to and are willing to work together. *People are what create businesses and people are what destroy businesses.*

UNDERSTANDING EMOTIONS DRIVES BETTER RELATIONSHIPS

I used to think when people "grew up" that they would leave behind thought habits which didn't serve them well like jealousy, anger, pettiness, lying, guilt, greed, spitefulness, and fear. What I didn't understand is that people don't leave behind habits which have served them emotionally.

One-half of the decisions that we make are from habit. Habits are created from patterns of thoughts over time.

When we think something works, we keep doing it even if the circumstances have changed. It might be important, for example, to cultivate enough anger to get out of an abusive relationship. Anger, after years of passiveness, might be the stroke of genius that spirited a woman away from danger and transitioned her into new opportunities.

One of my coaching clients, "Alison," had such an experience. After liberating herself from an emotionally abusive relationship when she became angry enough to throw a vase at her husband, grab the car keys and drive away, Alison formed a belief that anger was the answer. Later as she took on roles in leadership, Alison believed her anger was the propulsion that created urgency and therefore productivity on her team.

When Alison cursed with the tongue of an NFL linebacker, her team members snapped to attention. If she threw papers, pencils, or stomped out of the room, people hustled to make her happy. In Alison's mind, anger was the key to success.

Anger worked.

What Alison failed to recognize was that her employees and leadership team resented her. They watched the clock, cleared their desk an hour before quitting time, found ways to procrastinate, talked behind her back, told customers to look elsewhere, and kept their resumes updated.

Alison was afraid that shifting from anger to compassion would ruin her ability to run the company. In her mind, compassion was the weaker component. It was compassion that caused Alison to marry a man that abused her.

During our coaching sessions, Alison came to understand that it was never compassion that bonded the two of them together. It was something entirely different—the need for validation. Because she was searching for attention, to be fulfilled by another, her ex-husband's original obsessiveness and possessiveness felt like love.

Alison's anger came from the need to be safe because she found that anger was the only emotion that drove her forward. Compassion was a concept that she had not felt nor observed as a child, so in her mind, compassion was the weakness that created her pain.

Compassion, redefined as stability, worthiness, strength, empathy, gratitude, and safety, allowed Alison to alter the way she led, which grew her team's desire to collaborate with her and increased her team's engagement to 92%.

THE POWER OF THE WINNING FACTOR

Alison created a better culture through **awareness, which is the key to cultivating cultures where people play well together.**

This might seem like antithetical thinking, but the leaders I've interviewed for this book focused on themselves first and then on their teams. You might think that focusing on yourself is selfish and that selfish people are not great leaders.

Jim Rohn said, "Learn to work harder on yourself than you do on your job. If you work on your job you can make a living, but if you work hard on yourself you'll make a fortune." Jim didn't mean not to work on your business, but Jim knew that you could not create something that you are not. You must first become what you want your team members to be. *You attract into your life that which you are.*

If you squeeze a lime, what do you expect from the lime? Apple Juice? Cranberry Juice? Orange juice? NO! Squeezing a lime produces lime juice. When stressful situations squeeze you, which is every day as a leader, what comes out of you? *The only thing that emerges from you is what is within you.*

The same is true for your leadership team and your team members. The only way to create a better team is to create better people, which starts with yourself and then trickles down into every single team member.

Beth Ford, CEO of the Fortune 500 Company, Land O' Lakes, and I were discussing the power of the Winning Factor. Beth's mother was a psychologist and her stepfather, a psychiatrist who taught intellectual curiosity. From them, she learned to lead with three important characteristics:

1. What is grounded in truth?

2. Am I willing to believe that I am not perfect and live in that awareness?

3. Can I provide myself with moments of grace so that I can find empathy for myself and others?

Not only did Beth break the barrier of being a woman CEO in a farm business full of men and bravado, but she is only one of the four Fortune 500 CEOs who are openly gay. She was able to accomplish leadership at this company despite the observable distance between her and those she leads. The way that she accomplished closing the gap was through the realization that leadership is not a zero-sum game. You must bring other people along with you and enable them to succeed. According to Beth, if you live in alignment with the following three questions, then you are true to yourself and your team.

1. Does this align with my values and mission?

2. Is the work I am doing making a difference every day?

3. Does this decision align with a broader view of the people in our company?

Beth grew up with a family who discussed deep issues at the dinner table. They reflected, questioned, and honored deep curiosity. From this beginning, Beth was able to find the pathway that creates great leaders—the willingness to look deep within to find the best answers.

GROWING THE WINNING FACTOR IN YOUR TEAMS

It is one thing to grow yourself, which requires courage and determination, but it is another thing to invest in growing the Winning Factor in your teams.

During the first two years of my coaching career, it occurred to me that we had too much drama, and that drama created division and negativity. My assistant coaches and I constructed the idea to teach our players soul skills, not religious skills, but the depth of attitudes needed to reduce drama, making our team culture fun, enjoyable, and gratifying.

Once a week, we met with our captains to coach leadership skills. We went through a workbook together and assigned the captains winning success steps for the next week. Our leaders showed more empathy, responsibility, and accountability. Our captains stepped up their leadership game, but we still experienced drama. UGH!

Going back to the drawing board, the coaching staff decided that all team members needed to increase their **Winning Factor**, which is the way they perceived life, because perception is projection.

Reality is based on the perception of ideas you've gained since birth, and that is the way you navigate life.

If you believe that there is a glass ceiling for women, you will always find it. If you believe that your color is a barrier for promotion to CEO, then other people will block every attempt to get there. If you believe that other people view you as sick or a sinner due to your sexual orientation, you will find judgment in every job.

Our players needed soul skills to traverse life so that they lived more in happiness and less in anger, grief, and fear. In this way, we could spend more time focusing on basketball and less time resolving people issues.

But first, I had to become a better human being, which I discovered was a lifelong process. Developing your Winning Factor is a lifelong journey because your character is always evolving. Life causes you to contract or to expand. Sometimes experiences create separation from faith, religion, politics, family, or yourself and sometimes those experiences are the avenue to completeness.

Complete leaders are more than conservation leaders because the term conservation leader implies that forward progress is not on your agenda. Conservation leadership is necessary because safeguarding what has been accomplished is essential. AND, if you become more of a maintenance worker than a groundbreaker, frontrunner, or trailblazer, nobody will follow you. A leader who is not a visionary focus on learning through misery or aftermath, using hindsight as a guidance, paying a hefty price in the decisions made. A complete leader, arriving through the Winning Factor, questions, learns from the mistakes of others as well as their mistakes, unravels deeper self-awareness, and focuses on future knowledge.

DEFINING THE WINNING FACTOR

What exactly is the Winning Factor and how do you get there?

The Winning Factor is the ability to observe without judgment, to witness with forgiveness, and to accept yourself through the process of surrendering all parts of yourself that no longer serve you.

This process could be called self-awareness, mindfulness, consciousness, wakefulness, enlightenment, or emotional intelligence. All of those are true. Over 75% of the leaders that I interviewed exhibited a profound ability to talk about their mistakes, losses, and lessons with detachment and wonderment. They spoke about their old unconscious self with compassion and shared their transformation to wisdom with humility.

Carol Spector Riegert, SVP and CIO at Oxford Global said, "As a young leader I was so focused on the outcome that I ran people over in the process of reaching a goal." Because Carol was an anomaly as a woman in IT where 90% of the population were men, she felt pressure to prove that she was more than a pretty face.

Pressure, perceived or real, can cause us to focus more on results than our team members, losing connection to our team members on the way to increased production. Recognizing that she had lost track of her father's early childhood teachings, Carol remembered that the way to success was through lifelong learning. During her father's career as a teacher in both the secondary and university systems, he exemplified the importance of how grace given was grace returned and that students were his most valuable assets.

Carol sought deeper self-awareness so that she could grow her team. Building her Winning Factor, Carol learned the value of assertive communication, active listening, and asking better questions.

Two of her favorite questions to ask herself were:

1)	What are people talking about but not telling me?

2)	What can I do differently?

Through deeper self-reflection and assessment, leaders with the Winning Factor ask deeper questions, but more importantly, ask questions in such a way that people feel safe responding. For team members to feel safe, they must feel that the leader they are speaking to is nonjudgmental, trustworthy, and compassionate. Leaders must be free of ego, meaning free of the insecurities which create the need to be right, the need for attention, or the need to be superior.

In this space of the Winning Factor, the focus is completely on the team member. This ability, contrary to thinking, comes from the ability to focus on yourself first. You must fill your cup every day before giving to other people. When you begin a day with a cup one-quarter filled, it does not take long for the cup to become empty. Once the cup is empty, the ego comes into play, making it challenging, if not impossible, to give attention to other people, because you are in survival mode.

In survival mode, clarity is impossible, because long-term thinking has ceased. All decisions are based on immediate gratification even if that gratification has negative consequences. It might feel good to let our tongues loose on an insubordinate team member, but it could also be the gap that never again allows for a positive relationship with that individual.

THE SECRETS OF BRAVE BELIEFS
All leaders, even those who proclaim confidence, have moments of doubt. The difference between those who win and those who lose in leadership is the development of the Winning Factor which includes the ability to admit, confront, and conquer doubt.

During the 23 years that I coached college basketball, the number one opponent we faced was never on the opposite side of the court. The number one opponent we faced were the "lies" our players told themselves about not being good enough.

Upon departing collegiate coaching to enter the realm of leadership consulting and speaking, my perception was that executive leaders would be free of insecurities. *What I forgot was that people are people no matter their titles and that being CEO or president does not negate self-doubt.*

Doubting our abilities to achieve, we search for assurance through other people. When they fail to supply us with enough confidence, it is easy to fall into the victim trap of self-pity with phrases like:

- "Nobody recognizes my abilities."

- "Life has always been hard for me."

- "Other people have it easier."

Doubt leads to self-pity, anchoring us beneath our potential and grounding us in not-good-enough beliefs, which create self-fulfilling prophecies.

When we think we are not good enough, we fail, and when failure occurs, it is confirmation that we are not good enough.

This viscous merry-go-round won't slow down until we focus on and build our Winning Factor.

When we have not-good-enough doubts, they come in phrases like:

- I can't.

- I should/shouldn't.

- I must/must not.

- I ought/ought not to.

- I am not enough/as good as.

- You made me (which means we believe other people control our thoughts and our actions).

Living in self-doubt, our analytical and often misdirected head dominates our heart, the center of faith. Our heads, domesticated by fear-led beliefs from other people, convince us that we weren't born with the right DNA or don't possess enough will power. Our heart, our lifeline to the highest potential, speaks from confidence and brave beliefs while the head speaks from skepticism, suspicion, distrust, and uncertainty.

The ego, that piece of us, which is disconnected from our Higher Self, is the stress multiplier that forms distorted beliefs about who we are and what we can accomplish. The ego pushes theories of lack, unworthiness, and incompleteness, and if it grabs our full attention, exposes us to the lie that we are incapable of accomplishing our goals.

"George" hired me to help him discover the root of his incapacity to reach his required sales quota. George said he was great early in his career, but in the past six years he hadn't been able to receive the vacation packages and extra bonuses from reaching his goals.

Without prompting, George knew his issue. He said, "I've lost my mojo, my confidence, that belief that says I can kick ass and take names."

I asked, "When did you make that decision?"

George, eyes squinting, replied, "I didn't make that decision. It just happened."

"Then there is your problem."

George, confusion etched across his face, said, "What is my problem?"

I asked, "Who made the decision that you weren't good enough?"

"I didn't make that decision. I had numerous life obstacles that hit me one after another. First, my mother passed away. Then, my youngest daughter had troubles in school. My wife and I disagreed on how to manage our daughter, which caused problems in our relationship. When all that was going on, my performance dropped."

"Ah. So, challenges in your life created doubt?"

Rubbing his chin, George responded, "You want me to say that it was how I responded to the challenges that created my doubt."

I smiled. "No, I don't want you to say anything. What I want you to do is to examine why you once thought were great and now you don't see that same thing in yourself. How did you lose something that is innately yours?"

"What do you mean by innately mine?"

I replied, "We get confused in this world, thinking that we are smaller than we are. We were born winners, and then after birth, when people start telling us what we can and can't do, we accept their words as our truth. If you were to stay in the awareness that you were born a winner and that nothing—not one single life experience—can eliminate your right, then you would never lose confidence."

George said, "Hmm. It looks like I need to step back in the awareness that I was born a winner and that experiences don't steal that from me. What steals that from me is my interpretation of events."

"Exactly."

George decided that he was the author of his creations. Once he made that decision, he empowered himself to be the salesman that he knew in his heart he could be, once again receiving annual bonuses and paid vacations to Greece, the Galapagos Islands, and Bali.

IMAGINE THAT ALL THINGS WORK FOR YOUR HIGHER GOOD

Our heart, the center of us, our Winning Factor, is connected to a higher consciousness. Whatever name we call the Higher Self whether it is God, Jesus, Jehovah, Yahweh, Allah, The Universe, or The Source of All That Is, we are intimately connected to that Source.

Our Higher Self never leaves us. Our inner stress multiplier, aka the ego, believes we are separate from All That Is and are alone in this world.

When connected to our hearts, there are no questions about self-worth. Because we were created from All That Is, we are intimately connected to unconditional self-acceptance, a trait unknown to our inner stress multipliers. Self-acceptance drives action toward all that we desire. Our ego, disconnected from All That Is, deters progress convincing us that our actions won't matter and that we are not good enough to achieve our dreams.

Imagine that all things work for your higher good. How would you respond to challenges knowing that all challenges are in your path for an advanced purpose?

Would you find the power to continue? Recover faster? Experience less anger? Have more energy? Look for solutions rather than wallow in self-pity? Would self-doubt be erased quicker?

If all events were for your higher good, even if you couldn't imagine what that good might be, how would believing in that concept be beneficial?

Julie Mosely, CEO of J Strategies, and a client of mine, understands that even if an event seems horrible that you can find an unseen benefit. Julie grew up in a dysfunctional household with a father abusive in various ways. Julie could have let those years deter her from believing in herself. She could have become passive allowing others to abuse her in her career and in her personal life. Yet even in this darkness, there was light.

When Julie was eight, her mother became a single mom, who learned to tackle everything. She taught Julie the confidence to know that they could figure out any obstacle that existed. If the floor needed refinishing, her mother would read about it, ask questions, and learn how to do it.

Her mother taught her to never focus on the failure, but instead to focus on the lesson learned. Julie's mother titled her "the boss of the dogs" so that she could learn how to lead a pack.

Julie could have folded up her desires and dreams, focused on the horrible events of her childhood, but instead she chose to see the good from her mother's lessons and engaged in therapy to grow beyond her past.

She learned five major lessons in her childhood:

1. Be resilient.

2. Be financially free so that you control your future.

3. See failures as steppingstones.

4. Have confidence to be bold and take calculated risks.

5. Yet beyond any fear that could stop you.

Without these skill sets, Julie wouldn't have been capable of building a prosperous marketing business as a team of two women CEOs providing strategies for clients to thrive in public relations, government affairs, and community initiatives.

Her resiliency and ability to stand up for herself is necessary in the world of government officials where sexual harassment is common and pay discrimination is the norm. Julie still faces men who use their power as a control mechanism.

Recently, she asked a New York Legislator to sign a letter supporting legislation that he had signed for the past five years. His response, "I'll sign that letter if you will get a drink with me at 11 p.m."

Julie responded, "I'd rather not get this letter signed than be forced to have a drink with you. If the drink wasn't tied to blackmail, I might consider it. Please walk away from me now."

Her response, while valid, created a tidal wave of negative responses by congressional leaders who determined that she couldn't circulate the letter. Her willingness to stand up for herself made serving her clients challenging because she was blacklisted from getting signatures.

For many, this would have been a career setback, but for Julie, it was just another lesson. She said, "I've learned not to be reactive and go for the jugular. I can still be assertive and more deliberate in my responses without anger."

When we believe that all things work for our highest good, we search for the lesson and the opportunity. Julie used her early life experiences to reach for higher good. Her company, J Strategies, is based on compassion, inclusiveness, purpose, and passion. Her partner, Jaime Vendetti, and her believe in seeing the good in all people and supporting their team members in becoming aware of their potential.

When we are disconnected from the belief that all things work for us rather than against us, our stress multipliers insist we are less than. When doubts surge into our thoughts, our ego splits from our Higher Selves. Our inner stress multiplier has zero power when tapped into the faith that we are worthy and enough.

To slay self-doubt, multiply the Winning Factor through unifying with your Higher Self. Five ways to build soul skills are:

1. Self-Reflection/journaling.
   What am I pretending not to know?
   What is stopping me from what I desire?
   What do I need to move forward?

2. Meditation: observing and controlling thoughts.

3. Sitting in silence with yourself.

4. Living in curiosity: seeking the why behind what happened.

5. Practicing empathy for yourself and others.

EMPATHY IS A PATHWAY TO BRAVE BELIEFS

"Power without compassion makes you a dictator, and the way to compassion is through faith." --Captain James McCormick

Empathy is one of the soul skills that separate imitators from skilled leaders. We can't buy empathy or simply say that we have it. Empathy must be acquired through life experiences where failure was part of the process.

During my interview with Captain James McCormick, I was blown away by his compassion.

Captain James McCormick, USA (retired) earned a Silver Star, three Bronze Stars with a "V," three Purple Hearts, and a host of other medals and accomplishments.

On April 11th in 2004 during Operation Iraqi Freedom, Second Lieutenant James McCormick, without concern for his life, and subjected to continuous enemy fire, led a small team of soldiers to defend their logical staging area in Bagdad. Just a few weeks earlier, James had chosen to return to duty after suffering two separate gunshot wounds to a hand and leg and a third gunshot wound to his chest which was mostly absorbed by his SAPI-chest plate.

On that fateful day in Iraq with bullets flying past him and being hit yet two more times with enemy fire, James didn't retreat to camp. Instead, he protected an exposed part of the perimeter by positioning himself in the gunner's hatch of his M998 HMMWV. He gathered soldiers from various units to defensive positions.

Under substantial enemy engagement and suffering injuries, his men refused his offer to remain in camp, choosing instead to fight beside him. Not only did they stop the encroachment of the enemy into their camp, but they also traversed three times into heavy battle to gain needed supplies.

Despite incredible odds, they protected essential military resources, saved hundreds of lives, and inflicted heavy casualties to the enemy. What was the "X" factor of leadership where his men chose the possibility of death over life to follow their leader?

Empathy.

After terrifying situations in battles when reflection was possible, James would sit down with his team. Gathering them in a circle, he gave each of them a chance to speak about their experiences. At the beginning of the conversation, they expressed bravado, then they nervously laughed at their situation, and then they would breakdown into tears. James sat next to them, sharing, accepting, allowing all words to flow, and giving them the grace to cry as soldiers.

James understood that faith was the only aspect he had to move him through battle, because fear prevented action.

To step into conscious leadership is to acknowledge that fear is the opposite of all you are, because you were born to expand, not to remain stagnant. Faith is the ability to march toward your goal without knowing the outcome while connecting to the feeling of standing at your summit.

When the inner stress multiplier rules your life, guilt, a form of fear, is your whipping stick. Imagine if James felt guilty in the middle of the battle about not making the right maneuver or calling the right battle lines. How would that guilt affect his ability to get his unit home safely?

> ### *Beating yourself up or living in guilt does not make you better, it prevents compassion for yourself and others.*

THE LESSON THAT FREES YOU

Eighty percent of my coaching clients believe that if they beat themselves up long enough that they will become better.

Perhaps. With time. But how much time are you willing to sacrifice? Does beating yourself up reduce or increase capacity?

One of my coaching clients, "Debbie," is a financial advisor. One day, a client became infuriated with her for something that she warned him about, but he ignored. He lost money, reported her to the head organization, and filed an ethical complaint.

All day long Debbie beat herself up, searching for ways she could have done better. Maybe if she talked to her client in a different tone or showed him on paper exactly what was at stake, or if she would have called in a second partner to talk to him, the outcome would have been different.

When Debbie called me, I asked one question: "What else did you get accomplished today?"

Her reply was, "Nothing."

I asked, "How did accomplishing nothing serve you?"

Debbie answered, "It didn't."

"How did accomplishing nothing serve your other clients?"

"It didn't."

Debbie did what most people do. Instead of moving forward and learning from the situation, she wasted hours, attempting to come up with a perfect way to deal with an unreasonable client. Her stress multiplier tapped her unworthiness buttons all day long. Debbie learned that beating herself up served nobody, so she made the decision to be present to herself and others during challenging times. This one decision enabled Debbie to be more present for herself and her clients.

LIVING IN THE WINNING FACTOR

The gateway to all **that we want is through our thoughts**. Most of us allow our thoughts to rampage our lives without attempting to stop their pillaging. Our thoughts steer our actions which propel our habits. If we are unaware of the thoughts that transport us from habit to habit, then we are not in control of our lives. We are being run through a program which is in control of our behaviors.

The key, then, to winning in leadership and life is through awareness of the thoughts that are either moving us forward or taking us backward. Forward thinking is going toward what we want while backward thinking takes us away from what we desire.

When we reside in backward thinking, we live in regret, grudges, hostility, unforgiveness, grief, anger, apathy, and guilt. Forward thinking centers around courage, acceptance, reason, love, joy, peace, authenticity, and integrity.

Backward thinking feels heavy while forward thinking feels light. Light thinking is aligned with self-acceptance, confidence, and assertiveness while backward thinking is concentrated in self-doubt, judgment, and passiveness.

Paying attention to how we feel is integral to what we think. Our emotions are signals to the stories that we've accepted in our lives as truths. There is a difference between *a* truth and *the* truth. *A* truth is a thought we've been thinking for a long time without examining it. *The* truth is a thought we've elected to bring into our consciousness that aligns with positivity.

Both *a* truth and *the* truth are created by us. *A* truth is a story that was planted by somebody else, and we've rerun the story a thousand times so that it became a belief. The truth is the realization that we were born winners and that the only reason we don't live the life of a winner is because we accepted other people's truths as our own.

To shift this thinking requires the eradication of false thinking. Since false thinking is a habit, we must replace a new habit of thinking. Habits can't be abolished; they must be exchanged.

Removal of backward thinking is a five-step process:

1. Become hyper-vigilant of your thoughts.

2. Recognize forward thinking versus backward thinking.

3. Look for the triggers around your thoughts.
   An event.
   A time.
   A person.
   An emotion.

4. Recognize the triggers before they capture your thinking and cause the spiral into more negative thoughts.

5. Rewire the thought to make it more positive through changing:

   Your philosophy about life. (A philosophy about life might be that life is hard. A new philosophy might be that life is challenging so that you can evolve as a better human being.)

   Forgiveness. (Remaining angry at a time, event, or person doesn't change the outcome of what you've experienced, but it can make keep you stuck in that space.)

The Winning Factor is what separates those who do from those who wish; those who can from those who blame; and those who want from those who have.

As a leader, we are more than service providers and product makers; we are the pedal that propels the bike. We are the sail that transports the boat and the rudder that determines its direction.

Behind each successful team is a leader who doesn't accept the ordinary but urges for the extraordinary and who understands the difference between pushing from the ego, which creates stress and self-doubt, and propelling people forward through their Winning Factors.

WINNING SUCCESS STEPS

1. What are three positive habits that create a better working environment for you and your team members?
2. What is one habit that if you changed it, would make you an even better leader?
3. What is one thing that you should be more aware of about your company or team?
4. What is one goal that you've had for at least a year and haven't accomplished? What do you need to learn or do different so that you can accomplish that goal?
5. What are three thoughts that move you forward? What are two thoughts that move you backward?

WINNING TAKEAWAYS

- We define ourselves through our life experiences. We don't see life as it is; we see life as we are.
- People are what create businesses and people are what destroy businesses, so we must focus on our people.
- One-half of the decisions that we make are from habit. Habits are formed from patterns of thoughts over time. When we know our habits, we can change the decisions that are not benefitting us.
- Awareness is the key to cultivating cultures where people play well together.
- We attract into our lives that which we are. To get what we want, we must change who we are.
- The Winning Factor is the ability to observe without judgment, to witness with forgiveness, and to accept yourself through the process of surrendering all parts of yourself that no longer serve you.

- When we think we are not good enough, we fail, and when failure occurs, it is confirmation that we are not good enough.
- Our Higher Self never leaves us. Our inner stress multiplier, aka the ego, believes we are separate from All That Is and are alone in this world.

WINNING QUOTES

"You must keep yourself grounded and humble. The way I do that is farm, because the tractor doesn't care who I am. Mother Nature will rain on me or not. The world doesn't revolve around me. I am a part of the world."
Jon Tester, US Senator, Montana

"The number one thing that makes a person a good leader is the ability to listen to the people around them."
Kathy Anchors-Budd, President/CEO,
National Credit Union Management

"Don't do anything half-ass."
Mark Vergenes, President, MIRUS Financial Partners

"Remember that the person doing the work probably knows the work better than you do."
Maureen Niemiec, VP, IT, Internal Auditing, Flagstar Bank

"When you acknowledge and accept the gifts you were given from God, your gifts will bring you to the attention of the right people."
Michelle Foster, CEO/President,
Greater Kanawha Valley Foundation

"The question to hold in your mind is: What impact am I having on others?" –
Richard Maack, VP, APG Polymer

"Keep pushing yourself into the unknown. Stay curious."
Sam Hocking, Co-Founder, CRO

"There is a price to always being right; you don't get a seat at the table. When you tell other people 'I told you so,' that is why you don't get invited back."
Samantha Johnson, SVP and Executive Director, Customer Contact Center, First Citizens Bank

"To be a lifelong learner requires that you are willing to make the changes necessary, that you are willing to move sideways and not just up, and that you listen to your internal conversations."
Sandra McDonough, President, and CEO of Oregon Business & Industry (retired)

"The more that you do something, the more effortless it becomes so that other people assume you are just talented."
Sean O'Neill, Two-Time Olympian, Three-time USA Paralympian Coach

"Learn how to stand alone comfortably in what you believe."
Sheryl Hickerson, CEO of Females and Finance

"I used to think that I learned everything in college, and now I know I have barely begun to learn."
Takehiko Nakamura, CEO of Blue United Corporation

*"The most important sentence that I've learned as a leader is:
f I could be doing it better, tell me."*
**Ashley Wiseman, Executive Director of
Greenhouse Solutions Foundation**

*"Some people complain that life is not fair. Remember that it
is not unfair."*
**Bob Yates, Former SVP of
Level 3Communications, City Council Member**

*"Culture is about driving direct conversations. You want to
talk to each other and not about each other."*
Brad Scrivner, CEO, Vast Bank

*"Always think of where you need to be next and strive to get
there."*
Brian Lipscomb, CEO of Energy Keepers, Inc.

*"Leadership never gets easy because new challenges arise
every day. Your job as a leader is to rise to the challenges."*
Brenda Weatherby, Director of People & Culture, Weatherby, Inc.

*"Whenever you think you know it all,
that is a call for learning."*
Carrie O'Brien, CIO of J & J, retired

"A great leader is forever inquisitive."
Cori Cook, CEO, Veza Heath

*"Every day you've got to get up and ask yourself, 'Am I doing
what I love?' If not, you need to change."*
Craig McLaughlin, CEO, Extractable

*"When there is a lack of leadership, nothing happens.
Somebody must lead and lead in such a way that others want
to follow him."*
**C. David Kikumoto, Founder and Chairman of the Board,
Denver Management Advisors, Inc.**

*"The most important thing you can do is not to believe
everything your parents tell you unless they tell you that you
can do anything you want to do."*
Gary Glass

*"Be respectful and honest.
You owe it to people to tell them how it is."*
George Soule, Partner at Soule & Stull LLC

"You must have a larger cause than yourself to be a leader."
**Gordon Riggle, Member, Chancellor's A
dvisory Board for the Center of Leadership at UC-Boulder**

"Build an environment where people feel like they matter."
Greg McCall, Owner of McCall Homes/McCall Development

*"Success in your career has less to with results and more to do
with how you are managing the narrative."*
Hayden Thomas, Founder/CEO, Paird

*"Everything that you have and that you are is the result of
how you've chosen to understand your experiences."*
Jeff Walters, CEO, Community Financial Group

"Don't ignore mindset management. Be consciously aware of what is coming out of your mouth."
Jennifer Bagley, CEO, CI Web Group, Inc.

"Study the importance of attitude, because your happiness and success reflect your attitude."
Jim Strawn, President, Jim Strawn & Company

"Summarize yourself as a single word, 'teacher.'"
John Naber, Owner of Naber & Associates Inc.

"The pathway to success in my early leadership was that I too dumb to know that I was tasked with something that was perceived impossible. Once I managed the impossible, I learned that there are many ways through obstacles that other people cannot perceive."
John Felton, President/CEO of Riverstone Health

"Money is a by-product of success. You don't build with money in mind; you build with the solution for your customers."
Sunmeet Jolly, Founder/CEO, GROTU

"There is nothing more powerful than humility, because it means that you are never too big or too small for the opportunity in front of you."
Jeremy M. Evans, President of California Lawyers Association

"The only way you get ahead in this world is by creating value for your own people."
David Flint, Co-Creator and Chief Executive Educator, Value Creation Co.

*"People are your biggest challenges
and your biggest rewards."*
**Anne Warner Cribbs, President/CEO,
Bay Area Sports Organizing Committee**

*"A great leader has the ability to take feedback, either
constructive or positive, without affecting his confidence
levels."*
**Jose Quintana, President,
AdventGX, Founder of Innovation Underground**

*"Never be shy to ask questions for questions are the
pathway to knowledge."*
Atiya Hamilton, CEO, Blue/Green Marketing

*"Never underestimate a good walk outside and the
appreciation of each small victory."*
Jayme Hill, COO, Diamond Media Solutions Inc.

*"There are a million ways to become successful; you need to
be good at only one of them."*
Ken Baris, CEO/Chief Visionary BHHS Jordan Baris Realty

"Standing still never gets you to where you want to be."
Darius McDougle, VP of Digital Marketing, Antenna

CHAPTER TWO

Engaging And Retaining Your Dream Team

When leaders live in the Winning Factor, they construct authentic relationships, because relationships are the keys to engaging and retaining your dream team.

The word "authentic" is often used to describe relationships outside of business, because being authentic is linked to vulnerability, compassion, sensitivity, attentiveness, and unconditional love. These descriptors might feel inappropriate or even weak to a leader who is uncomfortable with emotions.

Yet, when we fail to be personable, to genuinely show up emotionally, our team members feel disconnected. They are uncertain if they are speaking to a real person or a facsimile. This disconnect is the reason why our team members will not come to us with the obstacles that are injuring their chances for success. We might never know the keys to motivating them, supporting them, or shifting them out of self-sabotaging behaviors.

While we must keep a boundary between our team members and our personal lives, what is the boundary between TMI (too much information) and CHS (closed heart syndrome)? Maybe you've met a person who replays their entire life history in a single setting sharing their most private moments. Before the conversation was over, you were ready to jump overboard even if it meant you must swim three miles to land.

They've invaded your personal space through their loose tongue. On the other hand, there are those leaders who never share a shred of their lives and seem to be separated by a moat, three dragons, and fifteen crocodiles.

Neither of these types of leaders find their way into the hearts of their team members. The separation between leaders and team is where lack of motivation, productivity, and engagement lies.

To engage and retain team members, we create and maintain authentic relationships. The five characteristics of authentic relationships are:

1. **Wingmaker**: Gives you wings to fly.

2. **Connection Conjurer**: Values and creates honest conversations.

3. **Value Virtuoso:** Sees value in you and protects that value when tested by others.

4. **Growth Shaman:** Cultivates that we can learn from each other.

5. **Hope Master**: Pushes you beyond your comfort zone.

THE WINGMAKER: ADVOCATES FOR THEIR TEAM

Wingmakers believe that the reward of being a leader is the success of their team members. They focus more on building their team than titles and money. They advocate for their team, enable career trajectory, and unlock hidden potential so that their team members experience success.

Chad Greenleaf, SVP of Client Services at Appsflyer, and I met to discuss the definition of the greatest leaders. Chad defined the best leaders as force multipliers, those who provide wings for higher and further flights. Chad said, "My responsibility is to get to know my team. What are their motives, fears, desires, and hopes? In this way, they know that I care and that I understand. We can then find the root to any problem through understanding."

To build wings begins with trust. *Team members must believe that our intention is to build a positive relationship where the value is in the relationship itself.* We cannot be focused only on what they bring to us or what we can offer to them. To create wings, both parties must understand how they can benefit one another. **If one person takes more than another without offering to give, the relationship is transactional and will leave one person depleted.** This type of relationship is eventually a dead end where people feel manipulated rather than treasured.

Creating positive connections requires asking questions that emote positive energy.

- What do you love most about working here?

- When you head to work, what is the one thing that makes your heart sing?

- Who is the person at work that brings laughter to your day?

Our brains tend to vacillate between two domains: the analytical and the empathic domains. The analytical domain is mission focused while the empathic domain is socially driven. When we utilize questions that are tuned to positive feelings, the person to whom we are speaking is more open to being influenced by us.

One of the most challenging traits to cultivate as a leader is to let go of the need to offer advice and focus instead on asking better questions. Leading our team members to self-discovery through asking great questions provides confidence and empowerment.

THE AH-HA MOMENT

When I first began consulting, I learned that talking wasn't nearly as essential as listening. One of my clients, "Joe," had the courage to tell me that while he loved the information that I shared that he often left our meetings feeling as if he didn't receive the information needed. He didn't want to be talked *to* or *at*. He wanted the opportunity to explore his thoughts and to learn what he didn't know about himself.

This was a turning point in my coaching where I learned to find the right questions so that my client felt heard, and more importantly, felt that he had discovered new knowledge about himself.

Joe knew that his thought habits prevented him from achieving greater success, but he didn't understand why his knowledge wasn't enough to create change. As a people pleaser, he avoided conflict and struggled with saying no to the requests from his peers. People used him in achieving their sales quotas while he wasn't achieving his own.

Joe defined the obstacle but couldn't find a solution. The solution was inside Joe, but at a place where he couldn't access. He needed a facilitator to guide him to the buried knowledge.

My role changed from a *coach who was giving quick solutions for everyday problems to a consultant who provided the means for personal development.* My challenge was to ask the questions that would unravel Joe's inner knowledge, which meant that I had to become a better listener and infinitely more patient.

As we worked through questions, Joe became more elated with each ah-ha. His confidence grew along with his willingness to make the changes that benefitted him. He learned the power of setting boundaries with his peers so that he made his sales quotas. Instead of conflict, he engaged in conversations, which led to more opportunities to lead others.

Being a Wingmaker means adapting to the needs of your team. After leading Joe to his answers, I made substantial changes in the way that I coached by asking better questions.

Some of the best questions I've learned to ask are:

- How is that a problem for you? In what ways does this present as an obstacle to your happiness, success, etc.?

- What would it be like if that was no longer an issue?

- What would you rather have instead?

To gain more clarity after my client answers a question, I continue to ask, "What else?" What else is problem for you? What else makes you feel doubt? What else stops your success? What else makes you sad? What else brings success? What else is a great quality? What else makes people love you?

Chad Greenleaf understood that high-level leadership was not about his dreams or aspirations; high-level leadership was about being an influencer.

> *It is not about what you know that makes a difference; it is about how that knowledge is shared so that other people can fly.*

THE COMMUNICATION CONJURER: CREATES SPACE FOR HONEST CONVERSATIONS

When interviewing Mary Kay Bates, CEO of the Bank of Midwest, I learned that she grew up with a grandmother who owned a restaurant. Mary Kay observed her grandmother's daily habit to meet and greet every customer at the door by name. Reflecting on how her grandmother melded connections with her customers, which created loyal and lifelong customers, Mary Kay fashioned her leadership style to embrace her grandmother's wisdom.

Mary Kay and her team increase their communication skills through reading books, sharing conversations about what they've read, and continuous trainings. Every Monday morning, she organizes a team huddle where The Bank of Midwest members share goals, obstacles, and accomplishments. She holds a monthly town hall meeting where all team members can talk about their toughest challenges.

Mary Kay understands that tough challenges are not meant to be avoided but to be addressed head-on.

To meet challenges head on, we *must develop relationships where people feel free to express their feelings and thoughts.* Teaching communication is essential because we learn our communication skills from our parents. Most of our parents didn't take a class on communication or read a book on it. Our parents watched their parents and imitated them. At a young age, when we learned our skills, we didn't stop to ask whether they were appropriate, nor did we evaluate them; we adopted them without further inquiry.

These are some of the skill sets that we learned at home and now take to the workplace:

- **The Blame Game.** "You are the one who left the oven on."

- **The Need to be Right.** "I know how to balance our budget."

- **The Temper Tantrum.** "You don't understand me!" Then slams the door and walks out.

- **The Silent Treatment.** Say nothing and more of nothing for days on end until the fight is forgotten or lost its sting, but the issue is never resolved.

- **Compliant Pleaser.** "You are right. I am wrong. Let's do it your way." Then harbors resentment.

Most of our team members probably don't possess the skill sets to have winning conversations, so they rely on what they learned from their parents. They only way to create possibilities for better conversations is to train your team in assertive communication skills, because they cannot do what they don't know. If they knew better, they would do better.

Assertive communication is the ability to hold boundaries, listen, admit mistakes, give credit where credit is due, be clear and direct, share honestly with compassion, be confident, and to respond rather than react. Assertive Communication is a skillset that all people can learn when they decide that it is beneficial to themselves and their team members.

The benefits of assertive communication include:

- More win-win scenarios where both people depart feeling as if they received a benefit.

- Feedback is welcomed and considered necessary for growth and success.

- Placing the ego is in the backseat which allows for more objective conversations.

- Defensiveness is put to rest so that all people can be heard.

- Gaining the opportunity to remain firm in convictions while creating flexibility in conversations.

Mary Kay understands that communicating effectively means that when she has a problem with somebody or something that she needs to address it with **empathy, clarity, and truth**. There is no room for hinting about an issue or using a roundabout discussion which leaves her team members' thoughts and feelings up to interpretations and rarely ends up in resolution.

The only way to keep on a clear path is to verbally paint the picture of what that path is, reinforce that path, keep people accountable to the path, and have the conversations when they stray.

Mary Kay is committed to teaching her team members the pathways to greater conversations, which leads to a happier work environment and greater productivity.

VALUE VIRTUOSO

We've all experienced that teacher, coach, band director, or boss who we would run through a brick wall for. They asked us to jump, and we didn't hesitate. They asked us to sell more, so we doubled our quota. They asked us to cut our budgets, and we orchestrated more money.

We didn't multiply our talents because our leaders were likeable; we became greater because they had our backs when our backs were against the wall.

You might call *having your back* bravery, courage, or doing the right thing, which it is, and very few leaders have that ability to put themselves in the path of danger to protect their team members.

We tend to COOB (cover our own butts) first, because we don't want to lose our status, job, or career. For those of us who are willing to take the risk, we develop team members who are loyal to us for decades.

The Value Virtuoso is a leader who deploys empathy habitually. This "soft skill" makes team members more steadfast, engrossed, joyous, resourceful, and willing to work together. When team members feel psychologically safe, they share opinions and failures, and debate ideas without concern about judgment. The more team members feel **psychologically safe**, the more likely they are to work better together.

Leaders who create safety are the ones who go to battle when their team is understaffed, underpaid, and overworked. They are the first to speak up when one of their team members has been misquoted, wrongfully called out, or blamed. They don't turn their back when times get tough; they get tough with the times.

When I first spoke with Richard Lowney, Co-Founder and CTO of MiEdge, I grasped that he was the type of man who lived from his values. Richard learned early in his career that supporting other people was the most important character trait that he could have.

Richard made a habit of creating relationship equity with everybody who worked for him, beside him, or across from him. He understood that supporting other people meant that you didn't look for a benefit in return. He gave with the mentality that giving was a gift, not a bargaining chip.

In 1987 Richard was in the process of taking his company public. They were about 50% subscribed when Black Monday occurred, which was a global, abrupt, brutal, and unexpected market crash. He lost $400,000. Despite the crash, he kept all his employees, and they never missed a payroll while Richard and his wife missed their paychecks, forcing them to take out a second mortgage on their home.

To take care of his team, Richard got SBA loans and received money from the Economic Development Center. He said, "Failure is not an option when people are depending on you."

Richard was most proud of the fact that he was in business as an entrepreneur for 40 years and he never missed paying his team members. When there were too many people for his revenue, he would keep them until he could find them a safe harbor. He believed that his obligation was to treat people right.

Many of the people who worked for Richard keep connected to him, because he offered value to them. He said, "I never worked for money. I worked because I loved helping other people." Richard sold his last company for 50 million dollars, and he is still in the business of helping people.

GROWTH SHAMAN: CULTIVATES SHARING AND LEARNING

Our mind is busy, producing thoughts like waves upon the beach. When one thought wave breaks and releases, another one takes its place. In these rolling thoughts, we spend about 80% of our time in the negative sphere, judging others and ourselves, comparing, labeling good and bad, and repeating the same negative thoughts hundreds of times. Our thought waves, if left unattended, slam labels upon team members and soon we treat them as we've labeled them.

The easiest way to disconnect from our team members is to place a label on them that doesn't allow them to expand.

In our eyes, they can never change so we can't see if they have creative solutions, good ideas, or new talents. Once labeled, we lose the capacity to collaborate or seek their points of view. We've made our teams less productive through negligence of thought awareness.

Growth Shamans are committed to seeking the best in our team members, surrendering all labels, and creating a superlative environment for success. Realizing that we don't have all the answers, we live in curiosity, listen to our intuition, and are comfortable with uncertainty.

Growth Shamans surrender to the idea that **learning everything is impossible, but learning every day is critical**. We know what we don't know and are comfortable with that awareness. Growth Shamans recognize that the universe is boundless and perplexing and far too vast for the human mind to fully grasp. We trust that every day is an opportunity for growth and that other people possess knowledge that we do not, so we keep open minds, ask questions, and reach for acceptance rather than judgment.

When we are more in touch with our intuition, we are more likely to trust the intuition of others. We can rely on statistics, facts, figures, numbers, communication, and our five physical senses, but we also respect that intuition exists. Through respecting our intuition and the intuition of others, we can find deeper forms of comprehension and answers that our rational minds neglect.

Growth Shamans are tranquil among ambiguity. We understand that the journey is uncertain, that we cannot see around every bend, that there are curves among the straightaways, and that the end is not always where we thought it would be. We trust that we are on the right pathway even when we must change courses, because we know the outcome is for our highest good.

The best leaders are those who embrace their inner Growth Shaman and teach others to do the same. We don't hoard the information that allowed us to become leaders; we share all our secrets with those we lead. We don't want hundreds of shadows who imitate us; we want people who are able to lead themselves through obstacles and toward goals. To do this, we become teachers of all that we've acquired while consistently learning more.

We want our team members to think, create, and expand. We want them to create through their experiences by moving beyond recommendations, guidelines, principles, and theories. We want them to observe, fail, reflect, and try again. The true Growth Shaman knows that only through a deeply personal connection with our experiences that our team members will shine.

GETTING BEYOND LABELS TO SUCCESS

During the discussion that I shared with Michael George, it became apparent that his success was the result of parents who saw through labels. Michael struggled with reading throughout his educational career. At age five, he was diagnosed with ADHD, which at that time was termed by the medical profession as massively hyper-active. The doctors provided his parents with prescription medication to calm him down.

After his first dose of medication, his family drove to watch his older sister play basketball. Michael was so limp and incapacitated that his parents had to hold him in their arms for the entire game.

His dad looked at his mother and said, "We will never do this to him again."

In elementary school, the teachers discovered that he couldn't read, so the eye doctor prescribed glasses, which didn't solve the issue. Later, Michael was diagnosed with dyslexia, but at that time, it was unclear how to support dyslexic readers, so he was forced to go to the trailers behind the school building where extra reading support was given. He covertly maneuvered his way to the buildings labeled as the "dunce" buildings by his friends, ducking his head, slinking between buildings so that his classmates wouldn't see him.

In high school, Michael made A's in science and physics and D's in all the other subjects. He was great at visual learning and understanding three dimensional relationships. Rather than reading books, he scanned them to gain concepts and applied those concepts to his exams. With this method, he was able to graduate from high school.

During his youth, Michael was fascinated with electro-mechanical machines, especially pinball machines. His neighbor ran the Northeastern distributor sales for Bally's, which sold and rented pinball machines. When Michael was 12 years old, he went to work for his neighbor fixing pinball machines.

Michael soon recognized an opportunity to run his own business. When pinball machines were pulled out of circulation due to malfunctions, Michael bought 20 pinball machines form his neighbor. His parents moved their cars out of the garage, so Michael had a place to store and work on the machines. That first year, he bought the machines for $25 to $75 each, fixed them, and then sold them for $300-$500 each. Imagine a 12-year-old dyslexic and hyperactive boy making a profit of around $8,000 in the early 1970s!

When pinball machines were replaced with other gaming machines and playing at game centers became popular, Michael arranged for a $25,000 loan to open a center. Before graduating from high school, he ran seven different centers and employed 50 people. When he sold his businesses before entering college, he possessed more money than the average person made in 10 years.

Through a common friend, Michael was introduced to Dean Kamen, who was inducted into the 2005 National Inventors Hall of

Fame, and who owns over 440+ U.S. Patents. After Dean hired Michael, Dean asked Michael to read over a rental agreement for new building and to mark anything that needed to be revised and bring it back to him the following day. Michael took the rental agreement home with him but knew that he was incapable of reading the several page document, fearing that if he told Dean he couldn't read that he would most likely would be fired.

The next day, Michael took the document back to Dean and told him that it would take him six months to read and mark the document, because he had a reading disability. Dean said, "I knew that. I wanted to see if you would tell me. I wanted a person who had integrity and a man who learns unconventionally. You've managed to graduate from high school and attend college with a disability. If you are going to work with me, you must think differently."

Dean knew that **the ability to think creatively and to utilize imagination was more important than being able to read at a certain level**. Dean didn't see Michael's reading struggles as a deterrent; he saw them as an advantage.

Michael's parents were Growth Shamans, refusing to see their son's disabilities and instead opting to grow his genius. Dean saw an inventor who thought creatively. Because Michael had the support of Growth Shamans, he has worked for and created companies worth millions of dollars. In 1995, he created a company called Interlinks Technology, which he later sold for 60 million dollars.

He helped Continuum grow from 43 employees to 1500 employees. Currently, he is COO with Invicti Security with the goal to grow the company from 1.2 billion to over 5 billion dollars.

Imagine if we could squash the labels of our team members. Could there be another Michael George out there just waiting for the right leadership?

HOPE MASTER

We have all been through life challenges which have injured our confidence, put our goals on hold and created the desire to hide from the world. Leaders who have evolved their Winning Factors recognize the signs of team members who have lost their sense of power and support them in finding their way back.

Because the nature of being human is such that people face emotional, spiritual, and physical trauma, our team members' physical and emotional health will change from year to year. The person whose long-time spouse left them for younger, more energetic partner will have a transition period of questioning, doubt, anger, frustration, or apathy. The same is true for people whose health was altered from a healthy exercise nut to a broken leg that won't heal, or the diagnosis of a chronic illness where life will never be the same.

When we are invested in our team members, we are there to support them through the challenging times. While we are not doctors, psychologists, or spiritual advisors, we are humans who have the capacity to empathize. We can gently guide people back into confidence where they can find their balance and resume a purposeful life.

Empathy is NOT the same as sympathy. Sympathy is feeling the same emotions as the other person, which brings two people to negativity. Sometimes we want the other person to know that we feel bad for them, so we say things that dwindle the possibility of feeling good even more.

- "That is terrible. I can't believe that happened to you."

- "How will you ever recover from this tragedy?"

- "Life sucks, doesn't it?"

- "Life is so freaking hard. It is just not fair."

Empathy is a connection with compassion where you feel the desire to support other people. Empathy is the key to authentic relationships and is defined in three different ways:

1. **Perceptive Empathy**: The capacity to identify and comprehend other people's points of view.

2. **Emotive Empathy**: The aptitude to experience what other people feel.

3. **Empathetic Concern**: The ability to recognize what other people need from you.

USING EMPATHY TO MOVE OTHERS FORWARD

If we understood the key to the empathy people needed from us, we could support them in feeling valued and understood. During my first year of consulting with leadership clients, "Lindy" called me to deliver bad news. We had been working together for six months to elevate her leadership skills for a possible promotion. She felt secure that she going to receive the promotion based on her last evaluation. Instead, they terminated her because they needed to make budget cuts.

Lindy was devastated. She was one of the best leaders in the company and had worked there for 7 years. Her teams out produced other teams by 20%, and she was one of the first ones on the chopping block. She said, "This is not fair, especially since I just received an incredible evaluation."

"I understand that this is a challenging situation. Share with me how you are coping."

Lindy said, "Not well...and if I really told you how I felt, you would be subject to four letter words and nothing else."

I said, "It is okay to vent for a few minutes and to throw out some four-letter words, and then we will talk about what you are going to do to recover and move forward."

Lindy smiled. "I knew that you wouldn't coddle me. I knew that you wouldn't be like everybody else telling me how sorry they were for me."

"I understand how horrible this has been for you. I understand that right now life seems unfair. I also understand that you are tough-minded, talented, and that you will find a way to go on."

"This is why I needed to talk to you, Sherry, because I knew you wouldn't let me feel sorry for myself. I needed somebody to tell me that I will make it."

"Grieving is fine and so is anger, but neither of those emotions are going to move you forward. What is going to move you forward now?"

"How long do I get to curse? I might not run out of steam for a few days."

"Will cursing move you forward or hold you to the past?"

Lindy said, "I really want to curse and throw rocks."

I said, "Who are you planning to curse and throw rocks at?"

"My boss, his boss, the building, their cars."

"How is that going to make you feel better?"

Lindy said, "I guess that depends on how good my aim is."

I laughed, "What if you changed your aim and your rocks? What if your aim was toward something better and the rocks you threw were the talents that you have? What if you threw your multiple talents at a new goal? What would that look like?

Lindy replied, "Hmm. I guess I can throw my talents into something better, but I have no idea what that look like right now."

"You don't have to know right now. The only thing you need to know right now is that you will survive this moment, and you will thrive in the future. What if you took a bunch of rocks and mark each of them with one of your talents, and then pile them up by your door? Every time that you walk by the door, pick up a rock and take that talent with you for the day. Imagine how that talent would play into something new. The next day take another rock and play the imagination game."

"Lindy grinned. Can I take the rocks when I am done with them and throw them at my boss?"

"As long as the throw is metaphorical and that what you've thrown your talents into is a new opportunity."

Lindy responded, "I am feeling better already,"

I felt sadness for Lindy, but sharing my angst wasn't what she needed from me. What she needed from me was the knowledge that she would make it and a plan for forward progress. Lindy decided to leave the corporate world and turned her talents to the restaurant business, where on any evening, there is a waiting line for her food and award-winning pies.

Hope Masters know what to say, when to say it, and how to say it. **We bring our belief in others to the light so that they can see the way.**

HOW EMPATHY ALTERS OUR CULTURES

Hope Masters see the miracles in day-to-day living and believe that miracles exist. To inspire hope into others, we must first believe in hope. Art Smuck, former President and CEO of FedEx Supply Chain, discovered early in life that a wrong turn could be the right one.

Art shared with me the story of how he was driving to an interview when he took a wrong turn. As he turned around, he saw a help-wanted sign in the lot where he was turning. He went in, applied, and got the job as a route driver at Ozarka (Nestle Waters). From this humble beginning, he became a market manager, a VP, a group president, and then a CEO.

Art worked for Herb Shear, who owned the logistics company, GENCO, and then FedEx Supply Chain. Herb, who had lost loved ones to cancer, believed that all his team members should be invested in preventive care, especially in terms of getting regular physicals. In 2014, Art went to the Cooper Clinic in Dallas for another physical. He felt great. He had quit smoking, lost fifty pounds, and was attending the physical as a victory lap for his dedication to fitness.

As he was waiting for his cardio test, Art thought about leaving since traffic was going to become heavy and he wanted to avoid the stress of bumper-to-bumper vehicles. He was close to walking out the door when a nurse appeared. She said, "Who is Smuck? Are you skipping cardio? Do you really think that is a good idea?"

Instead of walking out the door, Art took the test and discovered that he had a widow-maker heart condition. If he wouldn't have taken the test and gotten surgery, he would have been dead within 3-4 weeks.

When other people ask him about his heart condition—how he is not terrified every single day, Art says, "Every day when I wake up, my first thought is that I get to experience life again."

Because Art understood hope and how hope was the magic marker to our thoughts, he made hope part of his leadership. He gave hope in terms of empathy, compassion, and listening to others.

During his role as President & CEO of FedEx Supply Chain, Art made a habit of traveling for visits and Town Halls across 135 sites in North America. During a long string of site visits, Art and his team picked up on negative comments being made about the attendance policy. He talked to the SVP of Human Resources, and she suggested they ask more specific questions to the frontline teammates on their visits. Art asked her to take the lead on getting feedback, but she believed it might make more sense for him to hear the feedback firsthand. Art could have pulled his CEO card, informing her that he had assigned it to her, and she should handle it. Instead, because he had experienced life at crucial levels, he knew that he needed to inspire hope and partnership.

Art agreed with her plan making certain his routine over the next few site visits included asking specific questions about attendance. He was overwhelmed with the responses received, none of them positive. This feedback prompted Art to assemble a team from all levels of the organization to completely rewrite the attendance policy which removed outdated and punitive policies, and included language based on understanding and balanced accountability. He shared with his SVP how valuable her nudge for him to take the lead in hearing complaints had been, and how those conversations had changed his thoughts and approach. As a result of her insights, the work lives of over 12,000 teammates had been improved. Art conveyed to his SVP that going forward he would be leaning on her for ongoing advice.

Art created hope through his organizations, because he invested empathy with team members from every walk of life. He discovered that by taking the time to ask people at every level what they felt, saw, and experienced at the office that he kept his pulse on the company. More than that, he showed each person that they were critical to the success of the company and could be not only a catalyst for change but play a role in the design of the future.

WINNING SUCCESS STEPS

1. List three methods you utilize to build relationships where the value in is the relationship itself.
2. What are three questions you can ask your team members that are tuned to positive feelings?
3. Provide three ways you challenge your team members to develop themselves personally.

4. What are two ways you create relationships where people feel free to express their feelings and thoughts?
5. In what three ways have you created a learning environment at your workspace where labels are eliminated?

WINNING TAKEAWAYS

- When we fail to be personable, to genuinely show up, our team members feel disconnected.
- Team members must believe that our intention is to build a positive relationship where the value is in the relationship itself.
- Creating positive connections requires asking questions that emote positive energy.
- To gain more clarity from your team members, ask, "What else?" What else is a problem for you? What else brings you success? What else is a great quality?
- To address tough challenges, we must develop relationships where people feel free to express their feelings and thoughts.
- We don't multiply the talents of our team members by being likable; we double their productivity by protecting them when their backs are against the wall.
- Learning everything is impossible, but learning every day is critical.
- Once we label our team members, we lose the capacity to collaborate or seek their points of view.
- Authentic leaders bring our belief in others to the light so that they can see the way.

WINNING QUOTES

"If you want to get the most out of your team members, help them become better people."
Michele Redman, Head Women's Golf Coach, University of Minnesota (retired)

"To get your mind to slow down, sometimes you must ask a question that is completely irrelevant such as: 'Did you walk to school or carry your lunch?'"
Norman Kromberg, Managing Director, NetSPI

"Don't anticipate what your people are going to say. Listen to them so that they get the answer they need, not what you think they need."
Patti Leichliter, CFO/COO, Three Rivers Bank of Montana

"Leadership is not a title but a privilege. A leader's responsibility is not to the title but to the people on their team. We have risen to the opportunity to positively impact people in a significant way."
Peter George, CEO, Evolv Technology

"To get the most from your team, you must be able to breakdown difficult and complex situations which are mind-numbing into concepts that everybody can understand."
Ricardo Perugini, COO Pana metrics, a Baker Hughes Business

"Be passionate about helping people find themselves.
Ryan Lauderdale, CEO, Rypen Fitness

"We must get better at helping other people develop their superpower."
Susan Moffett, SVP, BCG Digital Ventures

"You must be able to take complex subjects and boil them down to one or two key points.
If you can't explain it to your grandma, then you haven't simplified your points enough. When you simplify quickly, everybody on your team can get involved."
Wayne Nelson, President, Stockman Bank

"Find the best people who are good people and train the hell out of them. Don't be afraid of losing them. Want them to be so good that you must fight to retain them."
Len Morrissey, Managing Partner at
Morrissey, Metcalfe, and Associates LLC

"When you focus on the right people and develop the right people, you will see growth as a company."
Joseph Fluder, President/CEO, SWCA

"The most essential thing in dealing with team members is to create a transparent relationship where they can have genuine, unguarded conversations with you."
David Bell, CEO, Alps Insurance

"You should be more of a coach than a leader which means you've got to be good at diagnosing what motivates another person—the thing that makes them tick.
David J. Jacowitz, President, Evolution Financial Group

"Never give up on negotiating. Find what you can agree on and go from there."
Dee Brown, Montana State Legislator

"Use influence rather than authority to lead your team."
Jay Tkachuk, SVP Digital Services

"Bring people in and surround yourself with people who are smarter and think differently than you."
Jeremy Cochran, President, Americas, Stein IAS

"As a leader, you must deliberately give permission to other people to bring their whole selves."
Jill Tomain, COO, Credit Union National Association

"A CEO must manage the people who manage people."
Judy Peppler, President and CEO,
KnowledgeWorks Foundation (retired)

"Don't be a transactional leader;
be a transformational leader."
Lenette Kosovich, CEO of Rimrock

"The best means to deal with challenging people is to allow them to speak first, listen, and respond to what they say rather than thinking you know the problem."
Mark diTargiani, SVP, Pacific West Bank

"Keep the idea in front of you what the long game is and that the long game matters."
Mary Ann Dunwell, Montana Senator

"You must show up with positivity, excitement, and happiness to lead your team to greater possibilities."
Seth Greene, CEO, Market Domination LLC

"Position your people for success and then support them in getting there."
Terrence Mills, CEO, Founder, Director, Veuu Incorporated

"Address the feelings before the facts. Ask them what is happening, and then diagnose the problem."
JP Pomnichowski, State Senator, MT

"You cannot lead by sending out memos."
Kim Meier, Co-Owner, Meier Family Chiropractic

"Don't overpromise but always deliver on your promises."
Dave Nguyen, Founder and Chief of Solutions, TRU IP, LLC

"Possibly the greatest thing you can do as a leader is to recognize somebody's heart and drive then help them step into their full potential."
Greg Katcher, Owner of CHAT of Michigan Inc.

CHAPTER THREE

Making Success an Adventure

How do great leaders evolve? Is it nature or nurture? Or both?

While some leaders are born with innate traits that direct their need to step up, pick the teams, or become the point guard, they must still hone their skills. The skills needed are charisma, determination, perseverance, courage, empathy, vision, humility, adaptability, *and the ability to make success an adventure.*

There is a difference in the way that leaders look at the world. The way that you perceive the world determines how you live in it. Einstein said, "There are two ways to live your life. One is as though nothing is a miracle, and the other is as though everything is a miracle."

Ordinary leaders do ordinary things, but to become extraordinary, you must seek the miracles within yourself and your team.

When we see the world through the lens that miracles don't exist, there is no possibility for vision or motivation to move forward. This mindset stops possibility before it can be imagined, but a leader who believes that there is limitless potential, moves their team members to accomplish goals that most people deem unattainable. *To move the compass toward miracles, the trick is to see life as an adventure of never-ending opportunities.* This requires faith in your abilities and training your team to have faith in their talents.

There are seven qualities that leaders can use to make success an adventure:

1. Revise Your Reality Assessment.

2. Emerge as a Visionary of Potential.

3. Develop into a Mind Yogi.

4. Fail Swiftly, Recover Faster.

5. Shift the Focus to a Bigger Purpose.

6. Bend with the Wind.

7. Blitz the Crisis.

REVISE YOUR REALITY ASSESSMENT

As we chatted during the interview, Thomas Bouchette, President of Citizens Bank, emphasized that reality is what you create. Thomas was raised in a small rural town in South Carolina by a father who could not read or write and a mother with a fourth-grade education. His father died after an extended illness when Thomas was 16.

By age seven, Thomas worked as a hander on tobacco farms in the summers. Before arriving at his paid job, Thomas completed his home chores on his family's small farm. Often his workday begins at 5:30 a.m. and ended after dark. His was paid $6.00 a day to bundle tobacco leaves and hand them to a stringer who tied the leaves to a tobacco stick which hung in the barn to cure. By working hard, he progressed to hanging the sticks and then to a cropper where he made $9.00 a day breaking off leaves in the fields and stacking them on a trailer.

He left the farm and tobacco fields at 15 to work at an appliance store. He was able to graduate from high school while working full-time. Without a college degree, he often worked two or three side jobs to make ends meet.

Thomas realized by age 27 that he wasn't going anywhere in his life, and he needed a better career to support his wife and their soon-to-be newborn, so he sent out dozens of applications which were promptly rejected. He applied to the Farm Credit Service as a loan officer convincing the president to give him an opportunity. Without a college degree, Thomas could only be hired as a trainee in the appraisal department. Thomas took a 35% pay cut from his current jobs and drove 30 miles further each day to create a new reality from all that he had known.

He observed that the lenders made more money, so committed himself to learning more about lending and within six months was transferred to the loan department. Within a year, Thomas was able to handle more transactions and close more loans than most of his peers who were all college graduates. Thomas believed they while were smarter than him, they could not out work him.

Thomas progressed from a loan officer at the Farm Credit Service to an entry level job at a bank. Once he became a banker, he charted a course that would lead him to becoming an Executive Vice President and Chief Credit Officer. He then set a new course to organize and create a bank as Founder and President/CEO.

Looking back, Thomas realized that he was not qualified to start a bank, but was able to find a pathway to success, because his father taught him to never quit and to finish what he started.

Thomas developed the philosophy that you can't wish away a problem; you must figure out what it takes to get to your goal and develop the skill set needed. He realized opportunity often arises from change and disruption. To find the opportunity, change must be embraced rather than resisted and an awareness must be created that patience and persistence are part of the solution-finding process. Thomas is proof that commitment, effort, and grit can win over people who are smart and qualified but not committed.

We choose the way we look at life, including the challenges that come our way. How we approach an obstacle determines how daunting it will be to overcome. We might need to alter our mindsets, attitudes, or our capacities to search for the good in every situation.

Reality is different for every human being because reality is a perspective. Whatever lens we look through is what life we experience. Some people see life as a continual problem, and they live in less joy, because they see more problems.

Leaders who see life as an adventure have altered their perception about life. They see possibility in every problem. They see freedom where others see oppression. They see loyalty when others see betrayal. They see good when others see evil. Some people might say that you are not living in reality if you are not seeing what is.

Leaders who believe that your perception is your reality say, "Reality is what we make it."

We don't pretend there are no obstacles or ignore them; we simply refuse to live in them.

Living in a problem means that you cannot escape it. The problem becomes who you are.

MOVING BEYOND SELF-IMPOSED DESCRIPTORS

One of my coaching clients, "Jeremy," wanted to move up the ladder from his current position as an executive director. Jeremy's dream was to become the chief operating officer. During our sessions, Jeremy explained his challenges: he was Latino in a mostly white profession; he lived in poverty for the first 18 years of his life; he graduated from a non-Ivy league university; and he was gay. In Jeremy's view, these real-life scenarios prevented him from getting his dream job.

Jeremy's definition of himself became his obstacle because he could not see beyond the way he described his life.

When I asked Jeremy who he wanted to be, he would answer something like this: "Nobody in this company who is openly gay is in the C-Suite." Jeremy didn't answer what he wanted; he answered through his perception of the obstacle.

Jeremy was living in "What Is," but "What Is" comes from the belief of what you've been trained to see. We are domesticated from birth about who we are—what our status is in comparison to others and how hard it will be to move beyond our status. While it is true that people who are born with richer parents tend to live richer lives, it is not always THE TRUTH. Many folks have come from poverty to find riches:

1. Oprah Winfrey, Television host and producer: now worth approximately $3.1 billion. She was born to a teenage single mother in Mississippi and didn't have running water or electricity in her youth.

2. Howard Schultz, chairman and CEO of Starbucks: $2.9 Billion. He grew up in government housing with a father who couldn't keep a job that offered money or respect.

3. Ralph Lauren, Fashion Icon: $5.9 Billion. Growing up, Ralph's family couldn't afford new clothes, so he wore his brothers' hand-me downs.

4. Larry Ellison, Oracle Founder: $61.8 Billion. Larry grew up in a lower-middle-class community neighborhood in the southside of Chicago in a cramped walk-up apartment.

5. Kenneth Langone, Co-founder of Home Depot: $3 Billion. His family was barely above poverty level with his mother employed as a cafeteria worker.

For Jeremy to succeed, he needed to get beyond what he had experienced and how he defined those experiences. *It is the story that we create around our experiences that cause our pain.* I asked Jeremy, "What is one story from your life that keeps you stuck in the life you are living?"

Jeremy shared with me the story about how other boys in high school taunted and bullied him about the color of his skin and his sexual orientation. I asked him, "Who were these boys? Tell me about them."

Jeremy explained, "They were all white guys who lived down the street. They were still poor but a little better off than us."

"Okay. What else about them can you remember?"

"They were athletes on the football team, but they weren't the best on the team. They were the substitutes that played on special teams."

"And what else can you remember? Were they good students? Did they go to college?"

Jeremy smiled, "None of them had good enough grades to get into college. I don't know what happened to them, but in my classes, they struggled passing."

I said, "Okay, let's rewrite your story so that you see it differently. Why were they judging you? What were they hoping to achieve through their bullying? If judgment is always about you and never about the other person, what does their judgment say about them?"

Jeremy's assignment for our next session was to write about each of those guys, to gain insight into why they might say or do what they did. During our next conversation, Jeremy could hardly contain his excitement over his epiphany. "They were all insecure. All of them. They wanted to feel better about themselves by putting me down, which they believed upgraded their self-worth. It wasn't about me at all."

Once Jeremy understood that his perception about his self-worth came from other people and not himself, he was able to see his worth differently. He changed his mind set and saw possibilities rather than problems enabling him to be considered as one of the top candidates for COO. At the time of this publication, he was in the running for the COO.

We get to choose the way we look at things, and the way we look at things is our reality. Our outer experiences reflect the stories we tell ourselves.

Tom Robbins, author of *Even Cowgirls Get the Blues*, wrote, "One has not only an ability to perceive the world but an ability to alter one's perception of it; more simply, one can change things by the manner at which one looks at them."

Because Jeremy learned how to selectively edit his thoughts so that the right perception created the right action. Jeremy became a thought adventurer rather than a thought obstructor.

EMERGE AS A VISIONARY OF POTENTIAL

Visionaries of potential look for the pockets of feel-good in any situation. While these leaders comprehend that life is not always going to feel awe-inspiring, and there will be days when humbling experiences occur, **they also know that looking for the good often results in finding it.**

When we alter our mindsets to that of an adventurer, we explore experiences that build our reservoir of wisdom. We are under no illusion that every day will be sunny with the perfect sunrise and sunset. We also know in those days that are stormy, bleak, and uninviting, there is an underlying message if we sit still with it.

Visionaries of the potential change our lenses when life doesn't line up perfectly. We identify negative thoughts and quickly flip them. We search for upbeat people to share events with and to help us remember our beauty. We recognize when we minimize our successes and quickly spin our thoughts and words to acknowledgement and celebration of our accomplishments. We remember that life is not a sprint but a journey, and that the journey is the essence of all that we will become.

When I was chatting with Tina Lucas, SVP/Asset Based Lending Manager of WaFd Bank, she said, "I am a natural optimist and seek out what makes me happy." In her earlier years as an auditor, she didn't search for what was wrong, she looked for the evidence. By making evidence-based decisions, she kept her mind neutral, not looking for what was wrong, but rather for what existed.

Tina said that it is easy to become jaded as an auditor, because people think of you as the bad messenger. Tina discovered that 80% of the cases she reviewed were not trying to rip-off the bank. Most people fell into two categories: 1) Their books were accurate, and the bank made an error; or 2) They made an honest mistake. Only 20% of the people were committing fraud.

Being an auditor increased Tina's ability to be a visionary of potential. Rather than trying to prove what was wrong, she found that if she kept an open mind and sought the good in people, that she often found it.

Finding the good can be daunting especially when the circumstances that you were born in were taxing, but that doesn't mean that you must remain in them. Visionaries of potential find ways beyond their experiences or in their experiences that move them forward.

FROM THE STREETS TO CEO
JeVon McCormick had reasons to view life as a victim. His father, William, was a pimp and a drug dealer who fathered twenty-three

children. His mother, Anna, was raised in an orphanage, and at the age of 17, was handed $20 and a suitcase and told, "Good luck,"

Anna, with no skills and no place to call home, found herself on the streets trying to survive when she met William who offered her a solution to starving. She became one of William's women and doubled as one of his many girlfriends.

When JeVon was nine years old, his mother was arrested for welfare fraud, and he was sent to live with his father who often abandoned him with one of his heroin-addicted prostitutes. When JeVon was twelve, he was left freezing in a thin-walled apartment alone with three younger half-siblings, all younger than five years of age. When nobody returned for three days, Jevon survived the only way he knew how—he stole food.

JeVon did whatever was necessary as a teenager to endure his childhood circumstances which landed him in juvenile detention three times before the age of 16. When he was being released after his third stint in youth prison, a corrections officer told JeVon, "Let me tell you something son. You come back here again, and you won't being going to juvie, you will go to MAN prison."

The idea of a prison worse than he had experienced scared JeVon so much that he cleaned up his act. He moved in with his uncle for fourteen months where he learned discipline, responsibility, and religion. At fifteen years of age, he was reunited with his mother, and they departed Dayton leaving his father and the negative influencers behind.

JeVon had every reason to be the victim and to blame his mother and father for his early life dramas and to be angry at the injustices of life, but instead he chose to view life from the vison of potential. He saw life as lessons making the most his life experiences. When I interviewed JeVon, what struck me the most was the peace he held about his past. He told me, "Life was a blessing. I learned how to navigate chaos, stress, and people, and I learned to never be in a position where I didn't know what to do."

Jevon learned entrepreneurial skills from his father's pimp business by observing how William treated his employees. William berated his prostitutes, cursed at them, demanded they deliver more money, and threatened them if they failed to increase their business the next time. JeVon said, "I knew at age nine that I could be a better entrepreneur than my father. If William would have treated the women better and allowed them to keep even some of the money when they did well, he would have doubled his business."

Jevon never attended school, so he was fortunate to get a job in the mail room at the insurance company where his mother obtained a position after her release from prison. While JeVon delivered the mail, he seized the opportunity to educate himself on the playbook of corporate America.

One day while delivering internal mail, he walked by a conference room where a sign was displayed that read, "Free lunch and learn. 401K." Wanting the free lunch, JeVon asked a lady in the hallway, "Can you tell me where Conference Room 401K is?"

After chuckling, the woman explained that 401K was about retirement plans. JeVon showed up for the free lunch and learned two of the greatest words he had ever heard—compound interest. His curiosity was piqued about how compound interested worked so he read financial books at bookstores and utilized the internet to grow his knowledge about stocks and investing.

JeVon continued his education by working at pay Payday Loans where his first job in the storage room matching deposit and printout records. He quickly proved his determination to excel by producing more records in a day than any other employee ever had. The owner, seeing Jevon's potential, elevated him to a new position overseeing records at his numerous stores. After working eight to ten hours, JeVon often remained in the offices pouring through materials learning everything he could. After nine months, the owner gave him the title of vice-president allowing JeVon to choose the region of his choice.

As Jevon noted, "Life is nothing but choices." He chose to view the positives of his journey, searching for knowledge through his life experiences. He became a lifelong learner, examining his thoughts, observing others, reading, and asking questions. He taught himself the stock market, how to scale companies, and to be a CEO.

Jevon is currently an author, speaker, multi-millionaire, and President and CEO of Scribe Media.

DEVELOP INTO A MIND YOGI

Many of the leaders interviewed exhibited the traits of a mind yogi, people who have examined their mind, questioned it, and learned how to use its powers to their advantage. When Jim Traister, CEO of The Digital Navigator, discussed the power of the mind with me, he said, *"What makes a difference is getting the ego out of the way."*

To get the ego out of the way, it is necessary to understand the ego.

The human body is composed of three outer divisions: the five senses, the mind, and the physical body. The inner part of humans contains the mind, the intellect, the consciousness, and the ego. The mind informs, providing us with a never-ending stream of thoughts. The intellect delivers a decision while the consciousness visualizes the decision. *The ego judges, compares, berates, contrasts, and evaluates.*

The mind provides data, facts, logic, and stats. The ego receives that information and creates chaos out of it. Because the ego wants to be in charge, it focuses on self-importance and being the answer, which pumps up false pride. Our egos can crush self-confidence in a nanosecond because it is based on outside validation which is impossible to control.

Our egos are self-sabotaging machines because the more importance placed on winning, the more our inner judge berates us, which creates frustration, loss of confidence, and eventually the feeling of unworthiness.

Jim's first big lesson about the ego was at the age of 32. After being in the restaurant business, Jim became the manager of Wholesale Bakery, a 70-year-old wholesale bakery business.

Jim had practically zero knowledge of the baking industry but thought as their leader that he needed to know everything and do everything, which was a form of self-absorption, aka the ego. As a young leader, he made the mistake of believing that all people should think like him and wanted what he wanted; therefore, through his commands, everybody would willingly and passionately step into every order given.

What Jim's ego shielded him from was understanding the needs and desires of his bakers. He had an Executive Baker that was forty years his senior and a highly skilled French Pastry Chef that had been trained formally as an apprentice in his home country. The more Jim pushed, the more the French Pastry Chef and his peers resisted.

One day as Jim was lamenting about how his bakers weren't following his orders, his administrative assistant, Cindy, told him, "Jim, if you want the bakers to do better, you need to understand their culture and where they are coming from."

This was an ah-ha moment for Jim, as he had never really stepped outside his own goal-oriented belief system to consider his managers and bakers might have different desires than his. The bakery wasn't all about him and his desires. He realized soon after consulting with his administration that other people were involved in the bakery, which meant he needed to learn about them and their needs. When Jim surrendered to the awareness that the most powerful form of leadership was not in commanding (which is the ego) but in listening and focusing on the desires of his people, the bakery increased business and profit.

From this experience, Jim learned that personal development was essential to being a great leader.

"Now I own my mistakes, thoughts, failures, and successes and focus on the desires of every person I interact with."

By taking 100% responsibility, the power for our lives is in our hands. Often, we look for a system, a prescription, or an instruction manual to tell us how to find the answer to a problem, but power comes through the realization that the answer is always within us.

Jim continues to be a coachable leader—to live with self-respect while understanding that there is always the opportunity to learn from and with others. The key to being satisfied, living closer to solutions, and understanding that life is an adventure is to live less in our egos and more in alignment with responsibility. When Jim was younger, everything was goal centered. He became a goal machine, imprisoning himself in the belief that he was not enough, because when he reached one goal, there was always another one after it. Switching his focus out of the ego, he feels good about his accomplishments, not fretting about the next one, and believing that whatever comes next is a good thing especially when serving others.

USING YOUR MIND YOGI FOR MORE POTENT THOUGHTS

We get caught up in our ego without recognizing it, because the ego comes in many flavors: insecurity, the need to be right, moral superiority, the demand for validation, controlling, and power-grabbing. The ego can blindside us quickly, and cause reactions which fail us and our team members. While our egos will always be a part of us, we can learn to recognize our self-sabotaging efforts so that we can shift to more beneficial thought habits.

During one of my coaching sessions with "Cariana," she said, "I don't understand how my mind works. I was meditating today, peaceful, calm, focusing on my breath, and out of nowhere comes a memory from 20 years ago where I was working late one night when a guy in the office comes over to me and starts cursing and yelling at me for speaking to one of his clients."

"And?"

Cariana said, "It was 20 years ago. I haven't seen or talked to him in 18 years. He has nothing to do with my life, and yet in the middle of my peaceful meditation, he slams me. Why?"

I said, "He didn't slam you. You thought the thought."

"Well, why the heck did I allow that thought to pop in when I was at peace? What is that about?"

I asked, "What did you do with the thought?"

"Hmm, I obviously didn't let it go. I judged myself for having the thought, then slid right into the memory, and then got mad at him all over again, and then got mad at myself for getting mad at the memory."

I asked, "How did that impact your day?"

Cariana sighed. "I was meditating to be calm at work, to open my mind to new possibilities and to start the day off right. What I did was take that memory and judgment with me to work. One of my team members asked me a question and I bit his head off."

"How did that work out for you?"

"Then I judged myself for being a jerk and felt bad all day."

"How did that work out for you?"

Cariana shook her head. "Well, it didn't. I was trapped in judging myself and then judging the judgment, then beating myself up for it, and then hating myself for all of it."

I said, "Our egos are designed to make us judge ourselves, then become the jury of our judgments. Once we step into the ego's pitfalls, we create grievances against ourselves and others. How can you move forward now?"

Cariana glared at me. "You are the coach. If I knew how to move forward, I would. I am talking to you because I am in this dreadful cycle."

"You have taken the first step, which is to recognize the pattern of the ego. The ego is designed to make us feel unworthy which often comes in the form of judgment against others and ourselves. What would the next step look like for you so that you stop beating yourself up and taking it out on your team members?"

Cariana said, "Hmm. Forgiveness of the guy?"

"Yes...and?"

"And forgiveness of myself for the entire cycle. I had a choice to have the memory and let it go. Instead, I dove right into it."

I said, "Yes. It is easy for us to listen to the ego and do exactly what it wants us to do, which is separate ourselves from what is truly in our best interest. Knowing that now, what are your next steps?"

Cariana said, "Continue with awareness, shifting from judgment to curiosity, and knowing that I have the power to move from one thought to the next, and to release judgment of myself and others."

"And what else?"

"I need to tell my team member that I am sorry and to let go of that story so that we can have a positive relationship and that he won't hesitate to have conversations with me."

Cariana continued to work with awareness, curiosity, and learning to let thoughts go that were not serving her. She created a culture of trust that was recognized in the company and other company leaders modeled their department after hers.

FAIL SWIFTLY, RECOVER FASTER

Most people understand that failure is not defeat, but few of us act along those lines. Rather than get back up and try again, we waste time berating ourselves or walking away from our goals.

Leaders who have mastered the idea that success is an adventure do not run from failure but welcome it. Failure for them is education—a divine element of success.

When we see success as an adventure, we grasp that there will be rivers of uncertainty to traverse. There will be corners that we can't see around, and mountains that appear too big to climb. We don't have the answer readily available to us, but what we have is the unwavering faith that if we fail that we will find another route. We know that each attempt has the possibility of a breakthrough, and breakthroughs increase our speed of implementation and our processes for production.

To be a great leader requires hard work, determination, and perseverance. One of the most important traits of leaders who see success as an adventure is the ability to persist through failures until our goals are achieved. *The faster we fail, the quicker we recover, the more we learn, and the more valuable we become.* This mindset is essential for any leader because it shows self-confidence and the ability to knock out looming self-doubt when taking on a challenge.

The alignment with vision and purpose provides the vehicle for the doggedness needed to get through tough times. You are guaranteed that life will present obstacles which block the straight line from your goal to the finish line. When you fully grasp that every goal worth having is filled with hurdles and that you have the capacity to crawl under, jump over, slap down, cut through, or move the obstacles is when your dreams move from hope to reality.

When I interviewed Paul Brady, the SVP and CIO of the Arbella Insurance Group, it only took three minutes for me to comprehend that Paul believed in the "fail swiftly, recover faster" adventure mindset.

Paul is known as a leader who is skilled at building high performance organizations through strong relationships with the capacity to adapt to change. Paul has a strong conviction for pushing through obstacles. Failing for Paul is part of the process, but quitting is never an option.

As a youngster, Paul fell in love with baseball. He wasn't exactly the perfect size for a pitcher at 5'9", but that didn't deter Paul. Throughout his high school career, he played shortstop and pitcher. While he wasn't the star pitcher on the team, he showed brilliance on the mound fearlessly throwing balls that many batters couldn't hit.

Paul was mentally and physically prepared for his senior year and the opportunity to pitch in more games. During his first start on the mound, Paul tore his ACL and dislocated his kneecap fielding a ball. Feeling his knee pop, he glanced down to see that his leg was bent sideways. Undeterred, Paul tried to hop up on one leg to throw the runner out at home but found that he couldn't stand. Lying on the ground, incapable of physically being in the play, Paul yelled instructions to his teammates to throw the next runner out at second base. His teammates, seeing his leg bent at an odd angle, stood frozen on the field, incapable of throwing the runner out, eyes as wide as the Mississippi River.

Paul straightened his leg, knocking the kneecap back in place finishing the inning on the mound. The next inning, the kneecap popped out twice before Paul surrendered to his injury, retiring to the bench. For most athletes that would have been the end of their career, but Paul rehabbed with the fervor of a fanatical overachiever and made it back to the mound for the final game of his senior year.

The injury harmed Paul's chances to earn a college scholarship, so he attended Bentley University because it was close to home where he could commute and save money. After two years of focusing on studies, his former high school catcher convinced him to play a little pitch and catch. Paul's passion for playing baseball returned. Mentally erasing his old injury, he tried out for the Bentley baseball team.

Forty other young men battled against one another on the first day of tryouts to win one of the twenty positions on the team. Most of those 40 quit after the head coach, Coach Felice, set high work expectations and ran them through challenging sprint sets. Instead of running from the coach's mandates, Paul stepped up to them and was awarded a spot on the team.

His junior year, after not playing for almost three full seasons, Paul's well-placed sinkers, fastballs, sliders, and curves gained him a 6-1 record for Bentley, which was the best effort from the pitching staff. During Paul's senior year, Coach Felice selected him on opening day to be the starter against Boston College. Pro scouts were in the stands to watch the Boston College pitcher, Brendon Nolan, but Paul, confidence high and maybe tad over placed, thought he could snag the scout's attention off Nolan to him pitching his "fast" ball at a "searing" 81 mph (A major league pitcher's average fastball is 91 mph and if they throw it directly over the plate, there is a huge change that a hitter will slam it over the fence.)

Paul set an NCAA record in that game allowing 21 hits and 19 earned runs in four innings, which is a record that no athlete wants to hold. When Coach Felice came out after a couple of innings to ask Paul if he wanted to quit, Paul defiantly replied, "No!" Coach Felice said, "Then I better bring out the catcher's gear for you to wear so that you don't get hurt."

When most student-athletes would have quit after being shamed on the mound, Paul continued to play baseball throughout his college career ending his senior year at 3-3 and his 5th year at 7-2, ending his three-year career at Bentley with a 16-6 career record.

The key in leadership is to realize when we've gotten ourselves into binds, take a step back, ask for coaching, recover, listen, and then act. Learn when our fastballs are going to be hit out of the park and avoid throwing it right down the middle of the plate. Focus on learning and growing.

Find the lesson in every situation whether it is to continue the same path, pivot, or completely abandon the path for a new one.

Understand that things will go wrong. Not everything we try will work. Some will. Some won't. So what? Something will work if we have the determination to learn from it. Live in patience and faith knowing that the next step will get us closer than the last step, especially when our mentalities are to fail fast and recover quickly.

BEND WITH THE WIND

There is a difference between bending with the wind and breaking. Those leaders who adopt a belief system that the most important thing is to find a **way that works best to get the right outcome** are more likely to win the goals of their company.

When we become inflexible and think along the lines of "Take it or leave, and my way or the highway," it often leads to the belief that there is only one exact way to accomplish a goal and our way is the right way. This belief not only leads to a waste of time, money, and a lack of innovation, but it also creates friction between us and our team members.

Bending is not the same as breaking. Bending provides us the opportunity to bounce back, go with the flow, or find a new path. Breaking is when being right is more essential than getting the project completed. Breaking creates fissures along team members, peers, and leaders. Once a connection is broken, it is far more taxing to complete ventures and to reach objectives.

We are concerned with excellence and quality assurance, which is the right mindset for any successful leader, but when we become ensnared with the method rather than the outcome, we lose sight of the right objective, which is to achieve the goal.

When we are concerned about perfectionism, we might say phrases like:

- This is the correct way to do this.

- I know how to do this.

- We need to follow procedures.

- The system always works.

- There is only one right way to make this work.

- We need to focus on what we've always done that works.

These types of phrases can lead to resistance, especially when we have creative people on our staffs—the type of people who think beyond systems and who will double our work output if given the opportunity. Some team members want the A-Z answers to get the job done. That is okay and needed, but if these types of members are the only type on our teams, they will be incapable of finding solutions and need our constant supervision.

One of the keys to seeing success as an adventure is to be in command of our responsibilities and making certain they are done correctly. However, to get the biggest results, step away from the need to be right and **transition toward the need to get the job done right in whatever way works best.**

THE RIGHT WAY IS WHAT BRINGS THE BEST RESULTS

One of my coaching clients, "Doug," the owner of a specialty company, told me that he spent 15 hours one day and another eight hours the next day putting in a new floor for his showroom. When I asked Doug, "Is putting down a new floor in alignment with your priority question? Is this something that only you can do in your company?"

"It is not in alignment with my priority and other people could do this, but I am not certain that the quality would be great."

I let silence linger between the two of us, then Doug said, "And, this might be a control issue of mine. I don't trust other people to do it right."

I asked, "What is the right way?"

Doug said, "Well, my way, of course."

We both laughed. Doug, like most of us, wanted his floor to be perfect, so he had to be the one to do it. As leaders, we are concerned about doing projects properly and correctly without snipping details or chopping corners. We want to follow systems, then rinse, and repeat. We believe in proven procedures that have been formed, analyzed, and demonstrated to work persistently over extended periods of time.

Doug was guilty of thinking that his way was the only right way to do something. While there are good ways to accomplish a goal, we don't want to get stuck in the belief that the only right way is our way. We need to learn the power of bending with the wind and learning that the right way is what works best.

Doug's concern was twofold:

1. He wanted to save money; and

2. He wanted to make certain that the floor was done correctly.

What we discussed about his decision that enabled him to alter his way of thinking were the following questions:

1. Was the money he saved worth the time invested?

2. Was he straying from his duties as the visionary of his business which kept him working <u>in the business</u> rather than **on** the business?

3. Was his way the only right way and could somebody else in his company accomplish the same task?

After our conversation, Doug concluded that his belief system around control and preferred method of excellence limited his ability to create and build a bigger business. Doug got back to what was essential—**working on his business rather than in the negligible details**, which was the key to increasing his sales.

While order and simplicity are important to the smoothness of operations, there can be variations of how order and simplicity are accomplished. Other people's ways may not be in alignment with your way, and their ways might allow for greater insights and innovations. The secret to bending is to make certain that your mission, vision, and value statements are clear, that your goal and project objectives are in alignment and then allow your team members the leeway to be innovative and creative.

The key is to think about the results wanted rather than the perfect line to obtain them. In the sport of Brazilian jiu-jitsu, there are no points for how to get your opponent to the ground, only that you take them down. Progress is slowed down by the need to be right, so spend less time worrying about how things are supposed to be and focus on the getting the result.

SHIFT YOUR FOCUS TO A BIGGER PURPOSE

Dan Pink wrote a book titled, *What Really Motivates Us*. Pink asserted that once a person had enough money that money was no longer a motivator. What really motivated us, according to Pink, was autonomy, mastery, and purpose. While autonomy and mastery are motivators, purpose is the driving factor that propels us from immobility to mobility. *By shifting our focus from a problem to a bigger purpose, we see the problem differently.*

There are times when we cannot think beyond the square in front of us, so we continue doing what we are doing, which might damage our departments, the organization, or ourselves. When we are stuck, we feel trapped which stimulates our flight or fight system. The more stressed we become, the less likely we are to find answers.

Shifting **focus to a bigger purpose gets us out of our survival thought patterns and into a bigger stream of inspiration**. Most of us began our careers with the idea that we could make a difference in the world but discovered that our desires got stymied in corporate or government systems. Falling into apathy is often the result of believing that what we do doesn't matter. To revive energy and propel action, the answer is in our focus.

When we feel anxiety, it is often a sign that we are focused on ourselves. When we shift our thoughts to service, a bigger picture emerges. We are now in the realm of providing hope, services, or products that will serve people, the earth, and animals. Authentically giving or thinking about others offers a lightness of emotions which lifts the burden of winning an outcome.

You've probably heard about the need to put on your oxygen mask before helping the person next to you or about making certain that you are safe before swimming out to help another. We cannot help others until we are in the best possible position to help them, but once we are at that level, we have the capacity to choose actions that come from our heart.

We must be aware that there is a difference between acting from self-interest and being selfish. Self-interest is the need to prioritize self-care before helping others, understanding that none of us chooses to do anything that is not beneficial to us at some level. When we volunteer our services, we are giving a gift of time and energy while receiving a feel-good emotion in return. When we offer money to charity, we feel buoyant about the support offered to others.

Selfishness is elevating our needs, desires, and wants above other people's safety, money, time, health, and relationships. While people can subconsciously perform acts in ignorance that negatively impact others, these acts are usually combined with an insensitive indifference to other people's pain, which makes them selfish.

We get ahead by helping other people get ahead, which is an act of self-interest (from our hearts) not selfishness (from our heads). By thinking from our hearts and not our heads, we've entered a different realm. The ego always stems from our survival brains while the heart offers us greater information. The heart is connected to our soul which has a greater capacity for information.

Jennifer Bertetto, President and CEO of Trib Total Media and 535media, acts from the heart, placing purpose above personal interests. When we were chatting during the interview, Jennifer shared that she didn't see herself as a leader at a young age, but she possessed one redeeming leadership feature—she cared about the success of each employee.

At age 25, she was a manager but not responsible for a team. Her skills were noticed by upper management who told her that they needed her as a leader, because she offered great insight. Jennifer ascended the leadership ladder to retail advertising director and director of sales until she was named CEO in 2015 at the age of 38.

The late owner was a billionaire who set up an employee benefit trust for the company in 2004. When he died in 2014, the company was losing 65 million dollars a year and seemed incapable of running for profit. The trustees who hired her believed they could control her, preferring her to continue running the company into bankruptcy, not wanting her to create a profitable company.

Because Jennifer believed that the employees were not just numbers, that they were real people, she had a higher purpose— to retain and serve the employees. Jennifer filled spots on the board with people who believed in saving the company and believed in her.

When the pandemic hit, they lost 80% of their revenue overnight before knowing that Payback Protection Program (PPP) was going to happen. The next morning, Jennifer met with the team and by 10:00 a.m., they had a plan to become 100% remote. Because Jennifer's purpose was clear—to always think in the best interest for her team members—she insured that nobody took a pay cut even though their hours were reduced by 20% pre-pandemic.

In 2021, Trib Media was voted best website for two years in a row and best newspaper for 3 years in a row and running for profit.

Jennifer met her challenges with a higher purpose, which enabled her to leave behind anxiety about her future so that she could focus on the futures of hundreds of others. When we live in personal survival mode, we cannot see beyond ourselves, but when we look beyond ourselves, more inspiration fills our thoughts and actions so that we can blast through the improbable.

BLITZ THE CRISIS

Leaders who believe that success is an adventure, don't wait for the right time to act; they act when the crisis is occurring.

They don't just act; they blitz the opportunity. They crash headlong into the crisis while other people are running or hiding. They don't haphazardly blitz; they blitz like a well-coached defensive football unit ready to sack the quarterback who is in position to score the winning touchdown. They know when to move, how to move, what areas to cover, and the most likely place the quarterback will throw the ball.

We must be prepared to coach our team to act on crises as they occur. Shying away from this moment will give the victory to somebody else.

The following are the keys to being prepared:

- Train our teams to look for opportunities rather than problems.

- Have clear goals established.

- Take consistent action toward our goals.

- Be prepared to step outside our comfort zones.

- Keep ourselves motivated through resilience training.

TRAIN YOUR TEAM TO THINK RIGHT

When we are in the problem, we can never see the solution. If a football defensive coach is only thinking about how the quarterback is throwing perfect passes, the coach cannot devise a plan to stop the quarterback. The focus is on the impact of the quarterback, which is more likely to result in a stream of curse words than a well-conceived plan of attack. The coach must shift his thinking toward the defensive options available to his team. The decision, then, is about which attack is the best one that will result in a win.

It is never enough for us to see the opportunity; we must train our team members to be able to do the same.

This is a conscious effort on our part to continuously talk about solutions, shift the conversation from the problem to the solution, ask for solutions, and NEVER EVER allow people to wallow in what-if-down thinking (spiraling downward into all the negative possible outcomes).

Marcos Peralta, SVP of Mastercard in Payments and Ecosystems, believes in getting impossible things done in ambiguous contexts. When I was interviewing Marcos, he told me the story of how we got his team to think right.

In 2019 Marcos was asked by his leaders to put together a new product development team composed of 50 product managers around the globe. The challenge was that more than half of the new team came from an acquired company. The new team members failed to flow with the culture and didn't like much about Mastercard. Marcos spent six months trying to resolve the challenges without any progress. Finally, he brought the product managers together, seated them in a big circle, and told them to write down the following:

- Two things you like about working here.

- Three things you don't like.

- One thing you've found interesting.

Marcos asked each person to read the answers they had written. He refrained from making rebukes or comments, and instead asked questions, listened, took notes, and probed for deeper explanations. It was a massive cathartic exercise putting the good, the bad, and the ugly in a pool of shared understanding. During this process Marcos discovered that many of the comments made sense and that several of the problems could be fixed with managerial courage.

After everyone had spoken, Marcos requested that all the papers be placed in the middle of the big circle. He asked the team: "Who came here today in cuffs as a prisoner?" When no hands were raised, he continued, "As I see it, as free women and men, you have three choices: 1) stay and fix what you don't like; 2) stay and make peace with what is; or 3) leave. What is not an option for you is to remain here in anger causing everybody else to be cross."

He looked around the room. "What do you want to do?"

When the managers responded, "Let's fix what we don't like," Marcos and the team began a transformation process that completely changed the internal dynamics and the team results. The product managers, released their past grievances against Mastercard, owned their destiny, and joined forces as ONE team. They saw the opportunity to win big and felt empowered to contribute to the solution. After that day, four new products were successfully launched in the market, and the team became recognized as a desirable place to work in the company.

HAVE CLEAR GOALS ESTABLISHED

One of the biggest mistakes we make as leaders is to have our staff establish goals and then never talk about those goals again until the end-of-the-year review. *Having a goal is different than making that goal tangible.* Goals can't be written down or stated once; they must be alive—seen, heard, and felt.

Making a goal dynamic means that people actively talk about their goals daily. They act on their goals—measuring, visualizing, reflecting, and sharing their successes and challenges. **A goal forgotten is not a goal at all. It is a wish that evaporated as soon as attention was removed from it.**

To make goals animated, we must write them on walls, on our email signatures, meeting agendas, and computer programs where progress is easily updated and noted. Use shareable computer programs like Trello or Asana where we and our team members can encourage and push one another forward.

Whether we are meeting virtually or in person, every day should start with a short huddle, stand-up, or what I like to term "Winning" meeting. In this meeting, the agenda is the following:

- A quick report on the status of current goals.

- If the goals were not accomplished ask, "What is your biggest challenge with the goal?" All members quickly provide their insights to move forward. This should not take longer than 10 minutes. If time elapses without an answer, the leader is now tasked to find a solution with the challenged team member.

NOTE: This is not a complaint session. Your responsibility as a leader is to keep the session moving forward in the right direction.

- Celebrate each goal completed with a quick high-five, shout, or series of claps.

- Establish new goals.

- Like any great team, end the huddle with a team shout or clap. This act reinforces team play and connection.

TAKE CONSISTENT ACTIONS TOWARD GOALS

A goal is a hope, dream, or a wish if action is NOT taken daily toward it. You will never find an Olympic Gold Medalist who said, "I am so lucky to be standing on the podium, because I never practiced." As a Two-Time Olympian, I worked out six days a week for twelve years to wear the red, white, and blue of the USA uniform. I ran thousands of miles, lifted ten tons of weights, practiced skills four to six hours a day, visualized, dissected videos, stretched, and carefully regulated my nutrition.

If we want to establish ourselves as a Corporate Olympians, we must drill for skill until the skills required are well sharpened. This is not a one-time thing; it is an everyday thing.

Taking consistent action toward goals means that our team members must be committed to the goal.

Most people remain at the interest level once they understand how challenging the goal is. They will find excuses to opt out. They will cite family problems, health issues, other work priorities, or that the goal is unreachable, and therefore a waste of their valuable time.

If they are interested, they will stop at the first obstacle. When they are committed, they will do what is necessary to complete the project.

Yes, sometimes people have a valid reason for not completing a goal. If you develop a sudden illness or have a debilitating injury, it might take months or years to get back on track. One of my friends—speaker, author, and professional barrel racer—Amberly Snyder, won the 2009 National Little Britches Rodeo Association All-Around Cowgirl World Title in high school and was prepared to continue her rodeo career in college as well as professionally.

In 2010, at the age of eighteen, Amberly looked down at a map on the seat of her truck. When she looked up, she was headed toward a metal beam. She turned her wheels to get back in her lane but overcorrected causing the truck to slide off the road, rolling the vehicle. Amberly was ejected from her truck, where she slammed her back against a fence post breaking her back.

After five hours of surgery, the doctors relayed to Amber that she had lost use of her legs and that going forward, a wheelchair would be her means of movement.

During the long months of rehabilitation, her physical therapist asked her what her goals were. Amberly replied, "Walk, ride, and rodeo," which became the title of her Netflix movie. While the therapist thought her dreams were ambitious, Amberly was committed to her goals. She was willing to do whatever it took to get back on a horse and to rodeo. Why? Because she loved being on a horse, feeling like one as they raced against time.

After only four months of rehabilitation, Amber was back on a horse. She returned to rodeo and rode in the professional circuit. While Amberly has not yet been able to walk, I wouldn't bet against her. Amber had a big motive to act consistently—she loved being connected to her horse and to movement. She wasn't going to let an accident determine her fate; she was going to find a way to do the things she loved the most.

BE PREPARED TO STEP OUTSIDE YOUR COMFORT ZONE

On Maslow's hierarchy of needs, safety is at the base of the pyramid right after our physiological needs. Before we can move up the scale toward love and belonging, esteem, and self-actualization, we need to feel safe. The idea of safety is never left behind as our subconscious mind is continually fueling the concept of safety to us. With every risk assessment, there is a deep-rooted fear that we will fail, and our subconscious mind needs convincing we will be okay. We feel fear when something unknown or new is in front of us.

> ***The difference between the people who are successful and those who are not is the willingness to feel the fear and do it anyway.***

New challenges provide new opportunities. Learning from failure and how to fail is essential to success. Remember that great leaders are not born, they are made from their willingness to evaluate, learn, and move froward from their mistakes.

Dean Bushey, Vice-President of Global Social Innovation at Hitachi, graduated from the Air Force Academy in 1988. He spent 25 years in the Air Force becoming a full Colonel where he acquired broad experience in unmanned systems, aviation, and leadership.

When Dean was in high school in Bloomington, IN, he applied for five different universities: Indiana University, Purdue, The Ohio State University, Illinois State, and the Air Force Academy. His single objective for selecting a college was the distance away from home. He wanted to create his life choices in a space unencumbered by friends and family.

Dean chose the Air Force Academy for three reasons: 1) he could play soccer; 2) his sister was in the ROTC and loved it; and 3) the Academy was the furthest from his home.

Dean had no idea how demanding the instructors were at The Academy. Basic Cadet Training was a six-week program designed to transform cadets from civilian temperament to officer mentality. Cadet training was grueling where young men and women were pushed to their limits physically, emotionally, and mentally. By the third week of basic training in Colorado Springs, Dean was ready to quit. He wrote a letter to his sister in the ROTC who had encouraged him to attend the Air Force Academy. He told her, "You were wrong about me and the Air Force. I am coming home."

He stayed one more week and then another and another until it was Christmas break. At Christmas, filled with homesickness, he once again thought that quitting was the best option. He told his mother, "I am not going back." His mother, undaunted by his statement, said, "Why don't you just finish the first year and then re-examine your options?"

Dean made it through spring break where he was no longer considered a first-year cadet, and he cultivated the habit of beginning his day at 5:15 a.m. attending military training, classes, athletics, study time, ancillary training, meals, and ending the day at 11:00 p.m.

When I asked Dean why he didn't quit, he said, "I thought about quitting many times, but in the end, I am not a quitter. I find a way through the obstacle." Dean's mentality comes from a winner's mindset: the belief that to grow, we must expand our comfort zone.

Doubt will come because doubt is an element of the human experience. It is what leaders do with the doubt that changes the outcome.

Later in Dean's career, after retiring from the Air Force, he failed miserably in his first four months in the corporate world where he treated his team members like they were in the military. His team pushed back. Rather than deciding the corporate life wasn't for him, he cultivated what he had learned from his experience as a first-year cadet: use a winner's mindset to find a way through all the obstacles.

Because Dean was confident in his leadership abilities, he didn't assume to know what changes he needed to make as a leader. He asked his team members how he could serve them better. He learned that they didn't need his micro-managing, what they needed was a leader who listened, asked great questions, gave them the leeway to find their solutions, and recognized them for their efforts and accomplishments.

Dean learned that living outside his comfort zone was the answer to triumphs. Risking failure was necessary for the rewards of achievement.

KEEP YOURSELF MOTIVATED THROUGH RESILIENCE TRAINING

Resilience is a result of both nature and nurture. Some people are born with grit, determination, and persistence, but those qualities can be deadened if past failure stops future progress. Resilience training is shaped by how we view adversity, which is learning to live through a philosophy that we control the way we think.

The Army has a ten-day resilience training program, Master Resilience Training (MRT), where they develop a soldier's capacity to conquer hardships and reevaluate challenges. MRT stresses viewing hardship as short-lived, concentrated, and controllable through mindfulness and willpower. MRT training includes seven modules focusing on: self-awareness, self-regulation, mental agility, optimism, connections, and character strengths.

As leaders, we cannot ask our team members to be tough if they don't know how to be tough. We must consistently train our team to have the desired qualities that create successful outcomes.

While we are impacted by our parent's thoughts, ideas, actions, and beliefs, we can choose to create a new blueprint for how we look at the world. This new blueprint can create a deeper resilience for overcoming adversity. Like the MRT training suggests, we can develop an optimistic outlook for the future. We don't have to settle for believing that life delivers us the worst-case scenario even if it is the way our entire family sees the world.

Resilience training ties into developing your Winning Factor. The more you understand yourself, the higher chance for transforming thoughts that no longer serve you.

Actively training our teams means that we possess a coaching mentality where training our teams is an everyday occurrence. Resilience training cannot be random or once a year. Like any great athletic coach, skills are rehearsed until they become habit and then skills are reinforced so they are not forgotten.

My top assistant coach departed our program after working with me for 17 years. I hired a former player of mine, Rachel, who outsmarted opponents with her game intelligence. She understood the game, anticipated opponent's moves, and practiced with intent. During our first year of coaching together, like every other year, we broke down skills from 1-on-0 to 1-on-1 to 2-on-1 to 3-on-2 to 4-

on-3 and finally to 5-on-5. Our system throughout the year was to break a skill down to the most basic form, then build it up to game intensity and speed.

During our first game of coaching together, Rachel turned to me and said, "Coach, the players are not doing anything that we taught them."

I said, "I know."

Rachel responded, "But we've been over this hundreds of times in practice."

"I know."

"They are NOT doing what they've been taught."

"I know."

Frustrated, Rachel said, "Then why the heck do we practice?"

I chuckled, "Rachel, they will get it. We just haven't practiced it **enough**."

This is the same mentality that leaders must have. If we want our teams to build resilience, they need to practice it.

The following are some of the ways to coach resilience:

- Do a weekly lunch and learn.

- Hire a coach/consultant to train your team.

- Designate 10 minutes each staff meeting to resilience training.

- Use resilience terminology daily.

- Email out weekly resilience winning success steps.

An example of resilience training would be:

- List ten factors that are out of your control.

- List five factors within your control.

- What changes when you focus on the controllable factors?

- List three emotions you feel when focusing on uncontrollable factors.

If your desire is to have a team who faces challenges with the eagerness of an adventurer, to explore the unknown with fervor, and to overcome any obstacle in their way, you must train them HOW to do this. Without skills, your team will fail when the going gets tough.

WINNING SUCCESS STEPS

1. What are three ways you can shift your mindset to see life as an adventure of never-ending opportunities?
2. List two action steps you've taken to help your team see the good in each challenge.
3. Provide three ways you've taught your team to embrace and learn from mistakes.
4. What are three methods for teaching resilience to your team?
5. What are two philosophies that will enable your team to blitz a crisis?

WINNING TAKEAWAYS

- To move the compass toward miracles, the trick is to see life as an adventure of never-ending opportunities.
- Extraordinary leaders don't pretend there are no obstacles or ignore them; we simply refuse to live in them.
- It is the stories that we create around our experiences that cause our pain.
- The faster we fail, the quicker we recover, the more we learn, and the more valuable we become.

- Those leaders who adopt a belief system that the most important thing is to find a way that works best to get the right outcome are more likely to win the goals of their company.
- When we get stuck in a problem, shifting our focus to a bigger purpose allows us to see the problem differently.
- Leaders who believe that success is an adventure, don't wait for the right time to act; they act when the crisis is occurring.
- It is never enough for you to see the opportunity; you must train your team members to be able to do the same.
- A goal forgotten is not a goal at all. It is a wish that evaporated as soon as attention was removed from it.
- To take consistent action toward goals, your team members must be committed to the goal.
- The difference between the people who are successful and those who are not is the willingness to feel the fear and do it anyway.
- As leaders, we cannot ask our team members to be tough if they don't know how to be tough.

WINNING QUOTES

"There is always an answer to the challenges in front of us. To find the answer, you must ask questions and invest in listening to other people's answers."
Leslie Ruyle, Executive Director of the Bush School of Government and Public Service/Research Scientist at Texas A & M University

"My biggest challenge was thinking that I knew everything and having to learn that even if I am right doesn't mean that I am right."
Mark Loftus, Head of N. American Consulting, Quest Global

"Don't fix the blame; it doesn't matter. Focus on constant communication, connecting often, talking about things before they fester, encouraging others, and sharing the bad news."
Sara Baxter, Global CFO, SVP, of Strategic Growth at Anaplan

"You don't have to be a subject matter expert to be a leader. What you must do is:
1) Ask questions.
2) Challenge your team members.
3) Support them.
4) Value their opinions.
5) Champion their ideas and empower them to find their own solutions."
Sheila Lamberson, Technology Manger, State Farm

"To resolve a problem; you must be motivated by the problem."
Shireen Yates, CEO of NIMA (retired)

"To hold your teams accountable, ask; 'Who, what or how can this get done outside of you?'"
Steve Ross, VP, Sales Development, Outreach

"I am innately curious. I like to know what makes things work. If I can find a way to do it faster, easier, and quicker, it buys me time to do something that I love."
Laurie Stewart, President/CEO, Sound Community Bank

"Keep your antenna up. Your career is 10% what you plan and 90% of taking the opportunities that come your way."
Barbara Morrison, Founder and President of TMC Financing

"One of the questions to ask yourself is: I wonder what I am wrong about? Then listen to your answer."
Bob Miller, President/CEO, One10

"Stop being the first person in the room to talk. Allow people to talk and listen to their ideas, questions, and challenges, then know when your decision point is."
Brian Waldron, President, and CEO, Dort Financial Credit Union

"You must find a way of professionally putting people in their place without being offensive."
Crystal Stanfield, VP Global Talent Acquisition, Cboe Global Markets

"Be true to your principles and integrity before being true to your job. If you lose your integrity, you've lost everything. If you lose your job, you will get another one."
Cynthia Persily, Vice Chancellor for Health Sciences at WV Higher Education

"A leader is a person with a vision and a focus on problem-solving with the capacity to get other people focused on how to complete the vision."
Dennis Custage, President, Global Boardroom Solutions

"To be effective as a leader, you've got to pay attention to everybody and become effective at managing up, down, and across."
Elaine McNeil, VP of Loreal (deceased)

"Don't tell people. Give them choices."
Jack Elder, CEO of Oregon Olympics

*"Be aware of your thoughts, because wherever your thoughts
go, your actions follow."*
Jeff Newgard, CEO, Bank of Idaho

"Get yourself a good coach who has done what you've
wanted to do and has helped others."
Jess Tiffany, Founder and CEO, MNU Digital

"One of a leader's biggest failures is lack of imagination
about the future."
**Jordan Goldmeier, Founder, The Money-Making Machine
Newsletter**

"People are more likely to follow you if you show
consistency from day one."
Kim Kaiser, CEO, Billings YMCA

*"Be prepared to step into leadership. Don't step into the role
until you've learned what being a leader takes."*
**Kimberly Miner, Chairman/CEO Envision You Victory Over
Violence Non-Profit Foundation**

CHAPTER FOUR

Champions Of Life

COURAGE DESTROYS FEAR

Many of your team members will lack confidence in themselves. They might pretend they have confidence while fighting back the insecure overachiever syndrome. Most of us have that little imposter voice inside of us wondering at what point our incapacities will be exposed. If your team is fighting internal battles, their external work will suffer.

Maybe your team members have heard "make fear your friend and not your master." Good idea...but how the heck can they accomplish that?

Fear will always be a part of life. It is not fear that creates damage; it is what occurs from fear—the interruption or disruption of goals, daily activities, and relationships.

Fear will arise when new challenges occur. Why? Because fear of the unknown outcome is natural and normal. Fear is part of the growth process.

Your team members might think that successful people don't have fears. To those who are struggling, successful people appear to accomplish their goals, live stress-free lives, avoid huge mistakes, and dive easily into new goals.

Not true. Everybody experiences fear. The difference between those who become champions of life and those who fail is the courage to acknowledge fear and act anyway. Champions make fear their friend and not their master.

A zero state of fear does not exist.

We will fear:

- Ridicule and rejection.

- Failure and loss.

- Abandonment and betrayal.

- Weakness and vulnerability.

- Heartache and pain.

- Unworthiness.

- Fear itself.

Even experts experience fear. When fear is in control, the outcomes are more likely to end in failure. Picture the number of WNBA players who miss the buzzer-beating shot, the NFL quarterbacks who overthrow the final- second-touchdown pass, the actors who forget their well-rehearsed lines, or Fortune 500 CEO's who make a career-ending decision. Did they fail on purpose? Of course not, but their failures were linked to faulty thinking, which is often birthed from fear.

A friend of mine, Aaron Lindau, was the first man to last eighty days on a solo trip across the South Pole on skis. During the first two weeks of the solo trip, he was deathly ill with bronchitis, and barely able to crawl in and out of his tent.

Aaron was able to navigate his illness plus broken sleds, ruined tent stakes, whiteouts, and weather conditions of forty degrees below zero. Imagine waking up to see white in every direction, and eating 6,000 calories a day, most of it butter, to survive.

I asked Aaron, "How often were you scared?"

He answered, "Every day."

I asked, "How did you deal with your fear?"

"I didn't think about it. I thought about how to survive and focused my energy on doing the necessary things to survive."

Aaron didn't focus on his fears. He focused on action.

Aaron's self-confidence was so strong that the dilemma of whether to acknowledge his fears wasn't in play. Courageous people admit fears and act despite them. Insecure people lie about their strengths, deceive both themselves and others, and blame other people and circumstances for their failures.

Aaron focused on production, not permitting fear to spin stories of what might happen, keeping his energy fixated on how to create a positive outcome. He wouldn't have survived eighty days alone in snow blizzards without the right mindset.

What is most terrifying are the stories scurrying through our minds about failure, especially when failure represents the belief that we are unworthy and incapable of success.

How many times did Aaron fail during his eighty-day trek? Almost daily. Aaron recovered from his mistakes, because he understood that failure wasn't his greatest fear—the belief of unworthiness was.

He could *recover from failure, but unworthiness would stop him from trying.*

BEING A LEADER OF LEADERS

Exceptional leaders coach their team members to new levels. We ask questions, listen, ask deeper questions, gently prod, acknowledge, praise, and request greater expansion. We accept people as they are and support them in realizing their maximum capacity.

To shift fears, we must provide a safe space where fears can be acknowledged. If we don't allow people to share their deepest secrets, then those fears go underground briefly before resurfacing to double their initial size. Whatever we resist, persists, so stuffing fear isn't the same as eliminating it.

The body is a vessel, holding emotions crammed into it until a similar fear arises. When another fear arises, it connects with the stuffed fears, causing an internal explosion, igniting our survival brain which freezes logic. By this time, fears have grown exponentially, paralyzing our ability to act.

The idea, then, would be to allow people to vocalize fear without assessment, judgment, or discrimination.

I interviewed Amanda Wiles, CEO of Enspire, and a dear friend of mine in the outdoor park at Fishtail, MT. Amanda said that she sees everything as learning and that she hopes her team can see and experience the world in the same way.

Amanda is a strategic optimist who is not naive about the world but believes that you cannot remain stuck in the problem, especially when the problem is fear. To move from fear to faith, Amanda listens to her inner guidance.

Amanda was a millionaire at the age of twenty-nine and then lost all her money two years later. Then, she suffered an unexpected divorce on Valentine's Weekend where she came home to an empty house where her husband took their money, half the furniture, and locked her out of their business.

She was completely blindsided by his actions. She had built, funded, and promoted the business out of love for her husband. Even though the financial loss occurred, she never realized that the financial loss could destroy the love between them. Amanda was shattered because love was the purpose and the core of her existence. Brokenhearted, Amanda lost hope in the human ability to love and felt as if there was nothing to hold her to this world. She laid down on the floor, empty and alone, experiencing the dead weight of hopelessness.

Even in her brokenness, Amanda was aware that she had a choice: she could succumb to greater darkness or expose her ruptured heart to God. She chose to open her heart to God, and experienced the words, "My child, peace. Be still."

In that moment, Amanda felt that she didn't have to do anything, but allow the presence of stillness, peace, and love. She felt the miracle of immediate completeness, where there was no pain or fear. She understood the connection with unlimited love was possible, comprehending that God was love.

From this occurrence, Amanda learned that her core reason for leading was to love and create opportunity for people—that it was the people she met in each experience who were her purpose. From her completeness within love, Amanda supported her team in facing their own uncomfortable spaces—the spaces of hurt and fear. Being in those spaces of hurt and fear with calmness and peace offered a space for healing where people could gain unlimited power to see and create their pathway forward.

"Everybody learns in their own way. The best I can do is to love them and offer options which support them in moving along their journey. If I talk 'at' people, they won't learn anything. If I am patient enough to ask questions, I offer a greater opportunity for people to understand the layers of their lives in a way that will positively impact their own journeys. My hope is to create opportunities for people to learn what is possible so that they can see and create their paths to success."

Amanda comprehends that in the workspace, fear is amplified by the speed in which we work to achieve our goals, and the time required to network, close a deal, or sell a product or service. Fear grows through questions such as:

- Am I good enough?

- Is this person better than me?

- Am I going to run out of time?

Amanda uses the following three philosophies to teach people how to move ahead of fear:

1. When you see a closed door, don't be afraid of it. Be willing to recognize it's a closed door and move faster to the open doors.

2. Use the breakthrough word, "And." This could happen AND what else could happen? The word, "And," allows for a step beyond the current fear because there is another option.

3. Amanda believes in focusing on two questions: a) What do you see when you are not afraid? B) What would you do if you were not afraid?

Fear can unravel us, throw us into despair if we allow its strength to grow without questioning its motives. The reverse is equally true—love can inspire and lift us with strength to create goals beyond what we have imagined.

When we stop to notice fear and understand that its power is in the underlying belief that we cannot achieve or have what we want, we can shift to be champions of life.

Amanda chose to view Valentine's Day a powerful day in her life. After experiencing the heartbreak from her first husband on that weekend, she now takes work off on Valentine's Day to experience love and witness all the love within and around her. Mike, her current husband, purposely proposed on Valentine's Day to create better memories around that day. Together, Mike and Amanda launched Enspire which was set to be acquired on Valentine's Day.

ACTION LEADS TO CONFIDENCE

To absolve fear, action is necessary. Fear itself is greater than the pain of failure. Failure we can get over, *but when fear stops us from trying, we have nothing to learn from.*

I visited John Assaraf at his home in San Diego. John built five multi-million-dollar companies, has been featured in eight movies, and wrote two New York Times Best Selling books. He currently owns Neurogym, a company which assists people with expanding their mental and emotional power to reach their fullest potential.

I asked John about his capacity to eliminate fear and live in confidence. He said that we are going to fear failure because we all fear failure. The people who act despite their fears are the ones who live their dreams. John loves to use the acronym, GOYA, which means **get off your ass**, because you cannot achieve without action.

Fear creeps into our thoughts daily. Our inner self talk can stir fear into a frenzy. Surrendering to our fears, we would remain at home, in a bubble, never moving, protecting our bodies, hearts, and minds from all threats. We would die without accomplishing a single goal.

One of my spiritual mentors, Bill Heinrich, author of *The Seven Levels of Truth: The Answer to Life's Biggest Question!,* informed me last time we spoke that he could read my future. He said "Your plans will either work out or they won't. Either way is perfect. If you let go of the outcome and believe that whatever happens to you is the journey you need right now, you are free to act."

In his book, *"The Book of Secrets: Unlocking the Hidden Dimensions of Your Life,"* Deepak Chopra said, "If you obsess over whether you are making the right decision, you are basically assuming the Universe will reward you for one thing and punish you for another. This isn't a correct assumption because the Universe is flexible-it adapts to every decision you make. Right and wrong are only mental constructs."

By accepting that we are fully supported in all choices, we are free to act. All options carry us forward to the journey of who we were meant to be. There are no wrong choices. Each choice provides a personal evolution. Some outcomes may not feel good, they but provide the wisdom to improve future results.

Fear is the opposite of our core; our true nature is faith. Fear prevents connection from greatness while faith encourages us to act with the knowledge that whatever action we take is moving forward to what we need to learn. Fear keeps us small while faith expands our possibilities.

Remember that ALL people feel fear and fear will ALWAYS be a part of you. *Decide whether fear will own you or you will own fear.*

USING FEAR TO MOVE FORWARD

Fear can be a tool if used correctly. Michael S. Segal, Merger Integration Specialist at Trust Bank, shared with me during his interview how he tackled the fear of experiencing 9/11 at the World Trade Center. Michael said that being positive was a frame of mind which he learned from his father during his formative years. His father often told him, "An excuse is like a crutch; it's only for the lame and weak." From his father's wisdom, Michael learned to let go of excuses, expunging the words, "I can't" and implementing the phrase, "How can I?"

Michael was notorious for being late never leaving enough time between meetings, and on the date of September 11th, 2011, being late was the miracle that allowed him to escape the fate that so many did not. He had a meeting at the World Trade Center on one of the upper floors of the North Tower. Because he was 20 minutes late, he was required by a security guard to stand by the side of the check-in desk to wait for a person from the meeting to come down the elevators to sign him in. During his wait, the first airplane struck the World Trade Center.

Hearing the loud crash and watching the lobby walls sway side to side, Michael was forced to dive to the ground when the airplane fuel exploded in the elevator banks and into the lobby. Aside from the person who signed him in at the security desk, no one is believed to have survived the meeting he was supposed to be attending. As he found his way out of the Trade Center and onto the street, he saw people covered in soot ashes, chaos in every direction, people screaming, and others falling from the tower. Michael, shocked, watched in disbelief as he realized the world's financial center was in shambles.

At this time, the fears of injury and death were exactly what Michael needed to get out of danger to find safety. Most people after experiencing a trauma of this magnitude would live in the trauma for days, months, or even years. Michael knew that the next best steps for him and his team members was to get back to a normal routine. He felt that focusing on the future rather than the past would promote healing.

On September 12th, he was tasked with getting the business back up and running. While he felt anger and sadness at the events of 9/11, he wanted to support those who survived and show the terrorists that Americans recover quickly with the never-say-die spirit that built our great country. He found an office building, secured computers and phones, and set up for the opening of the markets the following day.

He dialed into what his team needed from him. What were their fears? Their perspectives? What did they need to heal? He worked with his human resources department to provide support to those who struggled with emotional healing. He gave people time off to reflect, breathe, heal and the flex time to seek counseling.

After three months, Michael asked his team if they wanted to move back to Manhattan as a show of resilience and faith. They all agreed that the best way to put the fear of the past behind them was to step into the faith of the future.

Fear can be the right motivator when survival is at stake, but continuing to live in it prevents the evolution of our potential. Michael found a way to use his fear to move forward and to bring others along with him.

GET OUT OF THE SAFETY ZONE

Fear often leads to the inability of committing to a decision. When we sit in our offices, frozen, incapable of action, neither saying yes or no, we won't have that corner office suite for long. As leaders, we are decision-makers. People trust us to take the risk, to take the company forward, to be visionaries, and to lead from the front, the back, and the center. We must know when to decide and when to decide to do nothing.

Not deciding is the same as doing nothing which is different than deciding to do nothing.

One of my coaching clients, "Rick," was discussing a challenging employee. The employee used to be Rick's boss, had referred him to his current job, and was now under his leadership. Rick said, "Dave undermines our leadership team, steps over boundaries, and rarely listens."

I said, "So...why is Dave still employed?"

"Well, it is complicated. We've had a dozen discussions with him, and he hasn't changed."

"So...you've made the decision to do nothing?"

Rick squinted his eyes, creased his forehead, and responded, "No. We're doing something. We're talking to him."

"Has talking to him changed his behavior?"

Rick chortled. "No. We talk to him. Dave says that we're targeting him, gets angry, and doesn't change."

"Tell me where you've made a decision."

Rick asked, "What do you mean?"

"Did you give Dave an employee improvement plan and a deadline for change? Did you tell him the consequences of his behavior—what happens if he refuses to change?"

"No."

"It seems to me that Dave is making the decisions about his behavior and future in your company while you haven't made a decision."

Rick replied, "Ouch. That hurt."

I smiled, "The truth stings while a lie doesn't."

"Ouch again."

"Rick, you can decide to do nothing, do something now, or do something later. Those are decisions but doing nothing is allowing somebody else to run the company. Do you want Dave to run the company?"

"No. People would leave left and right. It would be a disaster."

I leaned forward. "Are people thinking about leaving now due to Dave's behavior?"

"People aren't happy."

"Hmm."

Rick said, "I see what you are saying. By not deciding, I am deciding to allow other people in the company to be upset and to eventually leave. I don't want that."

"Moving forward, what are your next steps?"

Rick closed his eyes, then opened them. "We need to decide to decide and not let Dave linger in this space anymore. We've got to give him a plan, a deadline, and tell him the consequences if he doesn't change."

"You are brilliant Rick, which shows up at a higher level when you reflect and take the time to determine what decisions need to be made."

Rick feared the outcome of losing Dave, Dave's anger, and the loss of his talent. Rick's fear prevented him from deciding, so he fooled himself into thinking that he had acted by having a non-productive conversation.

Once Rick understood the consequences of his choice to slide into indecision, and how doing nothing hurt the company, he had a winning conversation with Dave. Dave did exactly what Rick thought he would—blamed Rick, yelled, cursed, and threatened to quit. Rick said, "Dave, thank you for your time here. You can email me your resignation letter by tomorrow."

After Dave departed, tension in the department eased, employees became happier, and productivity soared.

We have three choices when it comes to decision-making. We can decide to do nothing which allows us to relax knowing that we've surrendered to the outcome. We can decide to take immediate action, with the permission to fail, which means we won't hold anything back. Or we can wait to decide, if time allows, so that we can weigh the outcomes. By deciding to decide, we're acting on our confidence that we are responsible for the outcome.

INCREASE YOUR POWER OF CONVICTION

Our self-images are concealed in the history of every event that we perceived went amiss. We lose confidence when we are oversensitive to setbacks, take them personally, and old wounds are kept open and bleeding. Those events have created a necessity for fears such as:

1. "I can't."

2. "I won't."

3. "I'll fail."

4. "It will hurt too much."

5. "I need to protect my heart."

6. "I won't survive."

Those fears are false perceptions. We might have been hurt in the past—used as a scapegoat by our companies, lied to by our partners, abandoned by our parents, or bullied by our peers. But, today, right now in this moment, those events are not happening. *The events are kept alive by our choices to revisit them.*

Heartbreaking events occurred, but they do not define us. Events cannot own our power or self-esteem. Take a minute to read the following questions. These are great questions to ask your team members when confidence is eluding them, because when *a false perception is awakened by the truth, the perception can no longer exist.*

- Are you suffering today from events that no longer exist?

- Are you holding onto the history of fear?

- How is your fear history serving you today?

- Do you believe that by holding onto the past that you can prevent future negative events from occurring?

- By surrendering your stories, will you lose self-definition?

- Are fears determining your next step?

- Are you safe being stuck in inertia?

Fears do not exist outside our minds; fears are events that have not yet occurred. Our connection to the emotion of past events links the belief that something bad might happen again. Fear makes us smaller, limits our talents, and prevents the lessons which enable us to become confident human beings.

The events of the past do not guarantee the suffering of our futures. We are the ones that guarantee suffering by allowing fears to prevent us from experiencing the present moment.

Moving forward requires letting go of past experiences that are creating false beliefs from the stories we've told ourselves. Aided by the knowledge that we are enough no matter what occurs in our lives, fear is erased so that we can act from brave beliefs.

VULNERABILITY AND SELF-AWARENESS ARE SUPERPOWERS

We cannot gain confidence by telling ourselves that we need to be more confident. That is like riding a merry-go-round believing that it will take us to New Jersey. We must take actionable steps to move into greater confidence. Winning a sale, creating a successful product, and increasing profits grow our confidence, and if we can't take the assertive steps to move into those wins, then we will never be confident.

It is the lies we tell ourselves that we need to confront. Hiding and avoiding truths about who we are is not the answer. Self-confrontation is scary because our limbic system responds to threats by going into survival mode—the state of fight or flight. Fight can be physical or verbal while flight is the act of running away through silence, disassociation, or denial.

Fearing survival, we search for protective mechanisms that provide a sense of relief. Denial is often used to avoid looking at realities that are too painful.

Tracie Kenyon, CEO of Montana Credit Unions, and I developed a friendship after her interview that has resulted in an ongoing zoom call per month. Each month, I am amazed by her intuition, compassion, and willingness to seek a higher truth. I asked her to expand upon the topic of the biggest lies she told herself. The following three paragraphs are what she wrote:

> The biggest lie that I have told myself throughout my career is that "I am not smart enough." I tried to assuage the lie by external education (bachelor's degree, master's degree and four professional certifications)... and guess what? The education would help for a while, but it didn't fully quiet the voice...because the trickster was still in there, needling me when I made an error, haunting me in my dreams, and chiding me during meetings. When I believed that lie, it limited my thinking, it kept me from truly leaning into my authentic self.

> To overcome the lie, I recognized it, called it out, and then I removed the word "not" from the lie. Now I tell myself, "I am smart enough." The recognition that I don't have to be the smartest person in the room was freeing! I only must be "smart enough," and I have always known that I am plenty "smart enough." To keep the lie at bay, I work on daily personal affirmations including Positive Intelligence® and spiritual meditations to build mental and emotional fitness. In addition, I engage coaches because what professional doesn't have a coach? Professional coaching has been a lifeline for me helping me to identify internal lies, build on my strengths, and set attainable goals.

> With my team, when I see denials, I encourage them to engage with professional coaches. It is critical to create a "safe space"

for difficult conversations and coaches provide that. Team members appreciate the investment of time and resources to assist them in becoming better humans, not just better employees. People show up at work with the emotional baggage that they carry in their personal lives; I believe that helping them to learn how to "unpack the bags" is a gift that will pay great dividends.

Through denial, the emotions of anxiety, frustration, distress, and overwhelm can be managed, allowing survival in "dangerous" situations or with "intimidating" people where we feel immobilized or helpless. Denial grants us permission to remain and operate in dysfunctional teams, unhealthy relationships, and toxic work environments.

The following are typical denials we employ to give ourselves permission to remain in negative scenarios:

Thoughts such as: *My boss, who is intelligent and wise, has been absent in his compassion and empathy for me in the past year.* A thought such as this often begins without much notice. We don't examine the thought before it builds momentum, often trying to justify our thoughts as we think them. We have the thought my boss has been absent in his compassion which shows up as demeaning or demoralizing comments, then we **justify** with: **but** he probably has had a rough year.

Concepts that: *Most corporate bosses need to be separate from compassion so that they can do their job well.* Once we have an unexamined thought, it is connected to a concept. Since we need to rationalize why we are being poorly treated, we attach our thought to a concept. Now we can explain why we are willing to subject ourselves to poor treatment.

Philosophies such as: *It is okay that my boss is demeaning and demoralizing, because he is the CEO,* *which means he is smarter than I am.* When we move into a philosophy about how our bosses are allowed to behave due to their titles, we will live in that same philosophy in other spaces and subject ourselves to continual mistreatment while denying ourselves the freedom to live unencumbered by negative people.

These thoughts, concepts, and philosophies are defenses which keep us in denial and prevent us from moving forward. We utilize defenses when we are fearful.

How do you know if you or your team members are living in denial? Listen carefully to the language utilized and the excuses given for people's behavior.

- I am not angry. *(After a person throws a water bottle against the wall.)*

- I don't hold grudges. *(After a person pulls the plug on a team member's computer.)*

- All I need is time to think through this, and I'll be fine. *(After five weeks of thinking.)*

- My boss didn't mean to tell me that I was lazy, stupid, and incompetent. *(When the boss has done this repeatedly for a year.)*

- My boss likes me. It is just that sometimes she gets frustrated with me. That is why she says those hateful things. *(After the boss has said hateful things for six months.)*

- My boss is a good man. He might drink and get drunk, but who doesn't? *(Too many people to count.)*

- I forgive people immediately when they wrong me. *(Says the person who talks incessantly about how other people did things to him.)*

- I will never be like my father/mother. *(Says the person who votes along the same party lines as his father did without examining her own beliefs.)*

- When I get out of credit card debt (lose ten pounds, make more money, etc.), all will be good. *(Until another desire creeps up on you.)*

- I know that our relationship didn't work before, but this time it will be different. *(After three separations and no counseling to confront the issue.)*

- My inner self-talk is always positive. *(When research has indicated that 80% of our thoughts are negative.)*

- I'm not like most people; I know when relationships are sour. *(Says the person whose partner calls her a dumb ass daily.)*

- I'll get help when I need it. *(Says the person whose plumbing project has taken over the kitchen for the past three months.)*

- I can quit whenever I want. *(After stopping and starting drinking 20 times.)*

When we use denial as a survival mechanism, the physical and emotional strain can result in self-destructive behaviors like smoking, overeating, binge drinking, excessive exercising, gambling, cutting, and self-medicating with tranquilizers and over-the-counter drugs.

When our emotions are denied, they persist until brought to the surface, faced, and released. Denial also has another cost—the repetition of dysfunctional patterns which were created by our protective mechanisms will be passed forward to team and family members, creating a whole new dysfunctional generation.

EXPEL FEARS THROUGH ACCEPTANCE AND PASSION

To become champions of life begins with overseeing our thoughts and understanding how those thoughts lead to actions.

The more confidence we have, the more we can share that conviction with our team members. The more self-reliant our team members become, the more innovative and productive they become.

Leaders can support others in finding their self-worth so that fears are drowned by the voice of worthiness. When I was coaching basketball, I often found ways to get players back on the track of self-confidence after a loss. I didn't believe in allowing them to find their way back, because that would take days if not weeks. They needed gentle prodding to remember how amazing their talents were.

We were ranked #3 in the country and #1 in our conference when we lost a game which dropped us five places in the national rankings. This was devastating, because it meant that we might lose the opportunity to host the regional tournament.

Like most people do when they fail publicly, our team members beat up on themselves. With heads hanging low, they came to practice thinking that the coaching staff was going to blast them for losing to an inferior opponent. They feared that we would make practice so difficult that trashcans would be placed in the corners of the court so that when their stomachs repelled food and drink from the punishing workout, they would have a place to throw-up without making a mess on the court. (This fear was totally unfounded but created by the belief that they would be penalized for underperforming.)

Knowing that our opponent didn't defeat us because they were better, but because we were fearful of losing our place in the national polls, we didn't need to punish our players on the court (which wasn't our philosophy anyway). What we needed to do was to refocus on our talents and to get rid of the fear that we didn't deserve to be in the top three nationally.

After a meeting with my assistant coaches, we decided the team needed closer bonding. We needed to expel fears with acceptance and refocus on how amazing we were.

At the team meeting, we gathered around in a circle. Our circle had the following rules:

- Each player and coach must take her turn in order.

- We are here in full acceptance of one another.

- There is no discussion or question after somebody speaks. We move on to the next person.

- The purpose of our time together is to get closer as a unit.

- We can laugh **with** you but not **at** you.

- There are no repeats. When somebody else says something, you cannot repeat what she said or repeat what you said in a previous round.

- You must start every sentence with the beginning of the question such as, "My biggest strength is _____."

For each question asked, we went around the circle ten times, giving each player an opportunity to find a deeper truth.

The questions we asked were:

- What is your biggest fear?

- What are your biggest strengths?

- Why do you love playing basketball?

The purpose of this meeting was to expose fears with acceptance and then to reinforce strengths plus passion. At the end of our circle session, I asked the question, "Will losing a game, cause you to lose your strengths or your passion for playing?" The answer was a resounding "NO!"

With fears exposed and confidence and passion renewed, we won the rest of our conference games, the conference tournament, and advanced to the Elite Eight, ending our season with a 31-3 record.

Fears don't go away naturally and if one member exhibits apprehension and shares that fear with others, the fear will grow throughout the team like a grass fire in a wheat field. Your responsibility as a leader is to discover where fears have interrupted talent, and to expose the talent so that the fears dissipate.

CONNECTING TO EVEN MORE CONFIDENCE

There are many pathways to confidence. To cultivate self-esteem, address fears so that they don't block progress. The more tools offered to your team members, the greater opportunity they have for success.

John Norden, VP of pricing at General Dynamics Information Technology, told me that confidence comes from focusing on all aspects of yourself. When things go wrong, which they often do, rather than sliding into fear, develop a Plan B, an alternative action plan. Later in his life, John developed type 2 diabetes. Rather than succumbing to the diagnosis and the fears of what diabetes could do to the body, John concentrated on the Four B's: body, being, balance, and business.

He looked at the body as fuel for energy created through movement and exercise. Being was the inner work of meditation, music, and journaling. Balance was focusing on key relationships in his life and making those relationships as positive as possible. The final "B" was business which was about learning and sharing. The confidence to conquer his diabetes came from a toolset that enabled him to shift from fear to action.

Some of your team members might have a low level of confidence without the tools to shift like John. While I believe it is always essential to identify the root issues and to teach people how to master fear, it is also important to coach your team where they are. Some people may not be ready to dig deeper, so coach them where they can make quick strides. Then, go back to help them understand how to be a true champion of life.

Below are some quick ideas to support your team in gaining confidence, because without confidence, everything is an obstacle.

- Record small wins daily. Have people share their wins every day even if the win is recognizing procrastination as a form of fear. Wins could be shared via an internet board, or a quick team call at the end of the day.

- Celebrate success. If your team is struggling, focus on what has been accomplished rather than what hasn't been done.

- Set small, achievable goals that can be completed in 24 hours. Rather than focusing on a long to-do list, which can exacerbate feelings of inadequacy, do things that provide a feeling of accomplishment.

- Have your team focus on their strengths and delegate their weaknesses. They will get more done if they focus on the things they do well rather than struggling with debilities.

- Allow them to have boundaries. They cannot say, "Yes" to all things and get everything done that is a priority. Make certain they understand their priorities so they can focus on what is most essential and say, "No," to things that are not.

- Coach them to subscribe to the idea that there are no stupid questions. Asking when they don't understand increases clarity which leads to greater confidence.

- Give them permission to talk about the elephant in the room. If they feel something is wrong but fear discussing it, they will withhold other fears. Sharing without fear of condemnation provides greater confidence for creativity and innovation.

WINNING SUCCESS STEPS

1. What are three philosophies you can utilize to help your team get past their fears?
2. What is the difference between not deciding and deciding to do nothing?
3. What are three questions to ask your team members which will support them moving beyond false perceptions?
4. What is one lie that you are telling yourself that limits your greatness?
5. List three ways to support your team members so that they can gain more confidence.

WINNING TAKEAWAYS

- Everybody experiences fear. The difference between those who become champions of life and those who fail is the courage to acknowledge fear and act anyway.
- Use the breakthrough word, "And." This could happen AND what else could happen? The word, "And," allows for a step beyond the current fear because there is another option.
- Failure we can get over, but when fear stops us from trying, we have nothing to learn from.
- By accepting that we are fully supported in all choices, we are free to act. All options carry us forward to the journey of who we were meant to be.
- Not deciding is the same as doing nothing which is different than deciding to do nothing.
- When a false perception is awakened by the truth, the perception can no longer exist.

- Moving forward requires letting go of past experiences that are creating false beliefs from the stories we've told ourselves.
- Without confidence, everything is an obstacle.

WINNING QUOTES

"Do not listen to people who tell you what you cannot do."
Peter Andrianes, Professor and Entrepreneur,
Co-Founder of Equarius Risk Analytics

"The bigger danger in conversations is not that they are misunderstood; it is that they are misconstrued."
Surjya Misra, VP, Client Services, Virtusa

"The person who is most hurt from your lie is yourself."
Suzette Turnball, MBA, Ph.D., Program Manager,
Higher Education Administration, Educator

"Have the self-awareness and confidence to build your team around your weaknesses."
Tim Flanagan, CEO of MassMutual Carolinas

"You don't need people who don't value you."
Timothy Alcorn, CEO of Alcorn Media

"You must learn to be okay with being unfinished, because you always have more to accomplish."
Tye Taylor, CEO Sunrise Media

"The characteristic of a dysfunctional organization is one where team members are afraid to speak up."
T.R. Romachandron, VP or Product Management, Velodyne

"It is okay to not do something perfectly, to redo it, or to ask for support."
Alesha Webb, President, Village Bank

"I believe in co-op-a-tition, which is cooperating while being competitive. They only way to do that is to put your ego aside."
Bill Klevenberg, CEO, Helpdesk

"Uncertainty is where creativity is allowed to forge."
Charles Dickens IV, Equity Compliance, Corporate Wellness, Consultant

"The biggest challenge that I've had throughout my career is myself—not getting in my own way."
Chris Green, CEO, Software Assassin

"You must be able to navigate uncomfortableness."
Christy Elliott, VP of BB&T, Charleston, WV

"Your imperfection is what makes you perfect."
Coralee Schmitz, COO of Rimrock

"The people who wanted me to succeed allowed me to make mistakes."
Gordon Pry, CFO of Sportsman's Alliance, Executive Office US Army Reserves

"I had an unwritten rule that I followed which was to never file bankruptcy. Find a way through the obstacle no matter what it takes."
Gregory Green, Co-Founder, Director, Equity Holder, Fatbeam

"You must understand your potential for greatness and then step into it every day."
Gregory VanDyke, Executive Level Leader, Stratify Technologies

"Be willing to let people go who are not working out."
James Binder, CEO, Co-Founder, Stiddle

"Great leaders understand their weaknesses and how to manage their weaknesses."
Jay Mattern, CEO, Villing+Company and TerraFirma Marketing

"You are only as good as what you've learned from your last mistake."
John Petrisko, Medical Director Employee Health, Billings Clinic

"The biggest challenge that most people have is getting out of their own way."
Juan Pablo Ogorio, Co-Founder Alpha Co Marketing

"As a leader, you must reserve the right to grow smarter."
Laurie Lachance, President, Thomas College

"One of the questions that leaders should continually ask themselves is: Am I showing up to get or to give?"
Marcella Gencarelli, VP, Manager of Client Engagement, Lakeland Bank

"Believe in yourself but always question yourself."
**Marco Sylvestre, Vice-President Product Development,
Venzee Technologies, Inc.**

"You have to lose the power of your mind to gain the power
of your heart."
Linda Patten, CEO, Dare2Lead With Linda

"Always remember that somebody is seeing something in
me that I am not seeing."
Samantha Howell, VP, HR, Hanes Companies, Inc.

"Remember that what you tolerate becomes the acceptable."
Jeff Heggie, Success Coach, Mortgage Specialist

"In order to seize your opportunities, you must recognize
that you don't know everything, admit your limitations, and
be vulnerable enough to ask for support."
Jeffrey Bissoy, Founder of the Plugged App

"Don't allow other people to manipulate how you feel about
yourself. Learn and grow. Become what others told you that
you couldn't."
Zaza Soriano, Interim CTO, TeleSMART Health, CEO, ZaaWink

CHAPTER FIVE

Collaboration Is The Doorway To Success

SEEK FIRST TO SEE THE EXPERT IN EACH PERSON

Rosandra Silveria, A Global SVP from a Fortune 500 company, shared her vision with me about how to create winning teams. She said the most important thing is to make all your different teams around the world believe that they are the same team. Rosandra said her superpower is "To impress upon our team daily that we is bigger than I and that us is bigger than me."

The key is to make each person feel valued and the way to do that is to not *care about your level or their levels, but to see people as experts in their fields*. Many leaders would agree with this statement, yet few of them can achieve the egoless state it takes to get there.

Rosandra is beautiful, wealthy, and a global vice-president with authenticity that bleeds from every pore of her body. She has managed to achieve success without the need for power or greed.

How does one achieve such a state? This is the work of the Winning Factors, the core of being beautiful from the inside out. It is the place where leaders don't need validation from the outside because they have formed a sense of worthiness from the inside.

When I speak about unconditional self-acceptance to Fortune 500 companies as part of leadership training, many of them struggle with the relevance of the topic. Why am I talking about self-esteem and forgiveness to leaders when they need to understand delegation, negotiation, and strategies?

The biggest obstacle to the success of an organization is people. The more leaders have aligned with their self-worthiness, the more they lead from a position of empathy. Why is empathy so critical? Because empathy is a quality of emotional intelligence. Emotional intelligence is important, because it is the number one indicator of job performance, leadership, and happiness.

When your team members are happy, they are more productive. The only reason that we have dreams and goals is because we believe that achieving those things will make us happy. We move toward actions that we believe will create joy and avoid actions that will make us sad, depressed, or angry.

Happiness might be defined as doubling productivity, increasing customer satisfaction, an upsurge in company engagement, or a decrease in diversity complaints. It could also be defined on a more personal level as a home, car, vacation, children, loving spouse, friends, or a fulfilling career.

What happens to leaders who chase goals without internal validation is that they lose sight of their connection with people, and once that connection is lost, happiness in the workplace dissipates.

To remain connected with people, leaders must continually connect with their internal values, which means constantly living in alignment with self-acceptance.

From that vantage point, the communication with our team members is different. We are no longer creating skip meetings for the sake of the meeting or listening without hearing. We can truly connect with people so that our meetings take on greater value.

Rosandra Silveria has taken one company in customer satisfaction from 60% to 90%. This achievement was not accomplished through dictatorship, power grabbing, or continuous needling. She achieved this incredible accomplishment through listening and validating ideas, bringing daily inspiration, and showing people how their belief of the impossible can change into a belief of the possible.

Rosandra doesn't throw out empty platitudes or hollow compliments. Her team members feel that what she says is true, so when she offers positive feedback, it is accepted without doubt. Individuals want to be around her, to step into her glow, and to feel her energy. This type of energy cannot be faked, and it is why her team members want to remain a part of her team.

Collaboration cannot happen unless we are in alignment with ourselves first. If we are in chaos, we cannot bring a team together in unity. Once we are unified within, we can see the good in each of our team members, treating them as experts and listening to their ideas with respect.

DIVING EVEN DEEPER INTO COLLABORATION

When we make the decision that collaboration is essential, we can create business structures that operate at the highest level of motivation: joy.

Richard Sheridan changed the way that he led when his eight-year-old daughter who had observed him working as a vice-president one day told him, "Dad, you are important. Nobody makes a decision without asking you first." His daughter's observations led to an innovative system of leadership where Richard created a no-boss infrastructure.

During our interview, Richard, CEO and Co-founder of Menlo Innovations, told me that while his daughter was the fire that lit him to change the way his company operated, but it was his father that taught him the early lessons that allowed for the innovation.

When Richard was 15, he went on an adventure with his Boy Scout trip into the wilds of Wisconsin. His troop of 15-and 16-year-olds were on a seven-day canoe trip where they were to learn navigation skills. During their trip, his father and another Scout leader had a disagreement about leadership. While the other leader wanted to take more of a central role, Richard's father said, "No. Let the boys lead. Let them make mistakes and find *their way out of them.*" During that fateful week, Richard learned that allowing others to make mistakes was essential to learning.

His daughter's observations taught him another valuable lesson which was that most organizations were held to the hero-based system where they could only scale the business if they scaled the hero. Richard, like his father, wanted a system where the team members were given more power and the opportunity to find their way and where the number one objective was to bring joy and happiness to the workplace.

Menlo Innovations is a company that designs and builds great software, but they achieve their results in a team atmosphere where there is no place for the word, "I." Their focus is completely on connecting with one another. Each member is paired with another member for a week where they collaborate on their software. At the end of the week, they switch pairs to experience new opportunities for creativity.

There are no individual bonuses handed out. Everybody receives the same amount for achieving the team's goals.

For this system to work, individuals must be capable of having diagnostic conversations with their partner. To show compassion, they ask, "Are you okay?" which allows for a more in depth look at the root issue. They are taught to provide other people the opportunity to change through observations such as "I saw this behavior yesterday. Would you like to reflect on that behavior?" Personal ownership is prized as are reflections and observations.

Team members learn to master their own stories and behaviors and how to work in pairs. The idea is to open the pathway to work heart to heart where people can share feelings and ideas without judgement.

HOW TO COMMUNICATE WITH ALL PEOPLE

Communication is the key to resolving all barriers that we face. Leaders acknowledge that communication is essential, so they create measures to communicate: town hall meetings, leadership huddles, skip meetings, and one-on-ones. While all these measures are essential, the key is not just in *the way we* communicate, but *how we communicate* the message.

You've probably met a leader who believed in an open-door policy. Their door was open, but once you got through the door, the leader was closed to your ideas, thoughts, and questions. This is the reason why so many leaders are unaware of silos, negative influencers, problems, and strategic downturns. They don't **allow** OTHER people to speak transparently with them.

We must do more than hold meetings; we must hold meetings where people feel free to challenge us and have honest conversations. If our team members know that they have permission to be right, to hold ideas in opposition to ours, and to question our assertions, then we are empowering our team members in the art of genuine communication.

When I sat down to interview Blake Howitt, Vice President-North America at SAP, he said, "Your responsibility to your team is to convince them of the truth about themselves that they don't yet understand."

Blake's father was a college dean, and his mother was a department head. He grew up watching how university administrators communicated and observed the challenge of it. Blake discerned that when you provided people with the right tools, they could go beyond the expectations of their roles.

The key, Blake said was to coach people where they were at so that you could understand what they needed from you. Blake said, "If you can't get where they are, you are not looking at yourself enough."

Genuine communication cannot take place without investing in self-awareness. If we are not aware of how our egos need defending and the triggers that prevent us from hearing what our team members have to say, then we cannot coach our teams to greater heights. Our teams become limited by our lack of personal development.

Like Blake so eloquently said, "To get to the leader that I want to be I have to look inside."

Blake believes that empowering conversation comes from the awareness that our leadership is not about us; it is about the success of our teams. When we grow ourselves to the point that we no longer need to feed our ego, we can make our first concern about how to resolve our team's challenges. Our wisdom will enable us to recognize that people aren't obstacles to our success, but unique individuals who need better tools to succeed.

What channels us into becoming the communicators who build bridges, create loyalty beyond measure, and grow Olympic-level leaders is the understanding that leadership requires the courage to overcome ourselves. In this way, we understand that our team members are not indebted to us, but that we are indebted to their efforts.

COLLABORATION IS THE RESULT OF PERSONAL DEVELOPMENT

It is easier to regulate laws, policies, and procedures than it is to regulate people. People are often challenging, because of how they've interpreted their experiences. If your team members have limited knowledge about emotional intelligence, they will bring their negative belief systems with them to work. These experiences can make it difficult to collaborate with others, because their insecurities create fear, which turns into controlling ANYTHING they can—their departments, projects, or other people.

Our responsibilities as leaders go way beyond getting team members to fulfill their job descriptions. If that is all we are focused on, we will get minimal results.

To get maximum results, we must be focused on building people rather than solely creating outcomes.

When we fail to grow our team members, we suffer from the transgressions of toxic teammates who do not validate themselves enough so that it is impossible for them to validate others. They wreak havoc in attempt to fulfill their emptiness. They shove obstacles in our paths due to the ways they view life. They don't believe that there are enough rewards, raises, honors, trophies, partners, or money to share. Since they don't feel good and don't believe they can live abundantly, they don't believe anybody deserves to do so.

Toxic teammates pretend to be sympathetic, compassionate, and encouraging to our goals, but they perceive that the good things that happen to other people thwart them from achieving their goals. Due to this faulty belief, they double their efforts to undermine every goal other people accomplish.

The quicker negative-minded people and their damaging schemes are identified, the faster we are released from their clutches and long-term effects of their manipulations.

We must acknowledge that some people, if given our permission, can steal our joy, passion, money, hope, and faith in mankind. When we learn to identify the toxicity of these teammates, we can have the conversations needed to either support them in altering their behaviors, or if necessary, terminate their services.

Become aware of the signals toxic people produce:

- You feel drained when around them.

- You feel the need to protect yourself.

- You feel responsible for their happiness or success.

- You feel that they are always in a crisis.

- You feel that you are not heard or seen.

- You feel that must sacrifice your needs and wants to get along.

Most people want to be good people, and most people have not done the personal work to escape some of their harmful behaviors. If their harmful behaviors have worked to their advantage, then it is twice as difficult to shift their behaviors. However, if we as leaders allow toxic teammates to continue acting in undesirable behaviors, we are injuring both them and our teams.

TEACHING MINDFULNESS TO ELEVATE UNITY

To avoid being controlled by manipulators, teach your team to become mindful of manipulator's traits— their quirks, faults, weaknesses, obsessions, and jealousies. Grow individual confidence so that negative influencers don't have the opportunity to sway others with their toxic toolbox.

Fixing other people is impossible—we can't make them happy or successful—but we can give them the opportunity to learn more about how to manage themselves and their emotions. Remember that other people's problems don't constitute our emergencies. *Focus on controllable factors—the ways we respond to their demands.*

When encountering negative team members, remember that our time and energy are for people who contribute and not contaminate us. Determine a time limit for interactions or cut ties completely. We must save emotional investments for ourselves and for people who genuinely care about us, our teams, and organizations.

Train your team members to believe in their worthiness so that no person can steal their passion. When they learn to validate themselves completely, toxicity remains where it belongs—on the person who needs to grow out of it.

The power in all relationships is to own our emotions, and to never allow other people to determine how we feel about ourselves. Nobody has the clout to make feel us feel sad, depressed, hurt, upset, or angry. We allow those emotions to occur.

MINDFULNESS CHANGES THE WAY WE SEE THE WORLD

While we don't own a magic wand that rapidly converts the mindsets of our team members, we possess the power of listening in curiosity and providing opportunities for our team members to hear their own words. We can influence the direction of their thoughts so that they see other possibilities. Some toxic thinkers are stuck in a mindset where they cannot see outside their negativity. If we provide them a new insight, they might find a better alternative.

During a coaching session, my client, "Bill," said to me, "I know that I don't have an easy personality, so it makes it challenging for other people to communicate with me."

I asked, "Do you want an easier personality?"

Bill said, "Yes and no. I want an easier personality, because I am often off-putting, making other people avoid me. Sometimes, they even call me names behind my back." "BUT" Bill continued, "My personality makes me emotionally strong so that nobody can take advantage of me."

I asked, "So, now that you are an adult and no longer in the situation you were in as a child, do you still need the old skills that got you through your earlier life, or could you find new ones that might make you more approachable and less difficult?"

Bill said, "But my skills work. Nobody takes advantage of me."

"So how is that working out for you? You have high anxiety, suffer panic attacks, and quit your leadership position so that you would feel less stress. Are those the skills you want to keep?"

"But if I become a softie, then people will run over me, and I won't allow that to happen."

"Bill, you can use a stick to dig a hole. It might take a while to dig the hole, but you can get it done. The stick works. Then somebody comes along and offers you a shovel. Would you take the shovel? Or would you keep the stick because the stick worked?"

Bill laughed. "So, what you are saying is that what got me here won't necessarily get me to a better place?"

"Yes, and one day somebody will come along and offer you a backhoe. The shovel will work until a more effective and efficient tool comes along. There is always a better tool, but many people hang onto their old ones, because that is what they know. Your challenge is to surrender old beliefs and replace those beliefs with better serving ones."

In our next coaching session, Bill said, "You are going to love this."

"What?"

"I carved a saying on a stick and put it in my office. The words on the stick say: Is this the best tool for the job?"

I laughed. "Tell me what you've discovered since the last time we spoke."

Bill said, "Well, I'm a lot less anxious because I know that more tools are available and what I've been doing in the past doesn't have to move into the future."

"So where do we go from here?"

Bill said, "Teach me more. Help me understand how I can become less difficult so that I have better relationships and less anxiety."

Bill remained a coaching client of mine for a year where he was able to reduce his medication for anxiety and move back into a leadership role.

GROWING YOUR TEAM COLLABORATION THROUGH REALIZATIONS

When I interviewed Steve Corsi, CEO of Volunteers of America Western Washington (VOAWW), he discussed how leaders are responsible for teaching that the hard can be easier. Steve believes that the biggest challenge in organizations is getting team members to believe they can accomplish their stated mission. To accomplish this, a leader must communicate that the hard is often a mental block. Steve stated that his main responsibility is to help people realize that more is possible so that they will work together rather than against one another.

Often the first response from team members for ambitious goals are: "We can't do it."

Once that mindset is established, the ability to reach the goal becomes more difficult. Steve teaches that the right thinking is not whether we can accomplish the goals, but how we can accomplish the goals. *Get rid of the "if we accomplish" or "whether we accomplish" and focus on the ways we are going to accomplish.*

Steve asks his team members why they think a goal cannot be accomplished, and then sets their sights on how to overcome those reasons. He said, "Most people don't know how to think through a problem, which causes them to stop at the problem."

During his 3 ½ years as CEO, Steve took the Volunteers of America Western Washington to the following growth:

- 17.2 million to 115 million in revenue growth.

- 342 employees to 685 employees.

- Opened a new senior center with 1,800 members.

- 34% growth in early childhood services.

- Built and launched a new teen center.

- Tripled their behavioral staff.

- Increased food distribution from 3.6 million to 7.9 million pounds of food.

- Opened a new food distribution center.

To get our teams beyond the negative and thinking of all the reasons they can't, utilize the process of winning brainstorming.

- Allow team members to introduce their concerns one at a time.

- Label their concerns on a flipchart.

- Ask the team to focus on solutions.

- Evaluate the risks of each concern from 1-10 with 10 being the highest concern. Anything below four is usually fear and can be removed.

- Focus on strategies for the concerns from 5-10.

As leaders, we are the answers to every objection. We are the light in the darkness. We are the teachers of right thinking. We are the reasons why the impossible becomes the possible.

Steve Corsi got incredible results because he believed that leaders are the conduits to greater insights and one of the best ways to increase his team members collaboration was to show them that the easiest road is often a dead-end road. When he forged ahead through the biggest obstacles and worked together with the right mindset, astonishing outcomes occurred.

FINDING THE RIGHT QUESTIONS LEADS TO BETTER COLLABORATION

Often the reason that obstacles exist is because we create them in our own minds. To get beyond our muddled minds, shift to asking questions that allow for solutions. We must alter our team members from complaining and imagining the worst outcomes to focusing on their abilities to overcome anything in their paths.

One of my clients, "Jabar," asked me, "What are the most essential things I can do as a new SVP to this company?"

I responded, "What do you think they are?"

"Darn it. I knew you were going to respond with a question."

I smiled. "Of course. What has asking questions taught you about leadership?"

Jabar said, "That I should ask questions first. If I make changes without asking questions, I will make enemies fast."

"Yes, and what else?"

Jabar laughed, "Keep asking more questions like what else is there?"

"Excellent. What is your philosophy on leadership?"

"What do you mean?"

I said, "Have you written a paragraph about your leadership philosophy-your beliefs about how you want to lead?"

"No. I haven't. I've thought about it, but never put them on paper."

"Okay, so why it is important to write your philosophy down?"

Jabar said, "There you go again. Asking questions to empower me, which means that is part of my philosophy. I want to empower others, to help them grow, to help them become the best versions of themselves. And, if I write my philosophy down, it becomes a contract to myself, something I can measure, and remember."

I responded, "Great. Get really clear on who you are and what you want to do. What are your top five values?"

"Another question. Hmm...the value of questions. That is a value: ask great questions."

"And what else?"

Jabar smiled. "Ask more questions of myself and of others. Be a coach, not a criticizer; lead with integrity; be a lifelong learner; have the courage to be wrong and to admit it; and empower my team to make the hard easier."

"Once you gain clarity on who you are and who you want to be as a leader, how does that support your team?"

Jabar answered: "I will not need their validation to make me feel better so that I can give them more. I will be there for them rather than asking them to be there for me. It will create better unity where we work together as a team, with them challenging me and me challenging them."

"Excellent. Now you have a starting point. Your challenge is to know your values and philosophy and stay with them. Review them weekly. Rate yourself on a scale from 1-10 with 10 being the highest number. In this way, you will keep your philosophy and values at the top of your mind. If you score lower than a 7, make a note to emphasize that quality for a week. Review your values and philosophy to see if they need to be revised."

Jabar said, "You are demanding. LOL!"

"I am not the one who will reap the benefits of your efforts. You are. You and your team. Always lead with values first and you will always feel good about you."

"And I will have more to give. What I want to do is to make a difference, to make the hard easier so that people can step into their greatness."

"Jabar, you are wise and thoughtful, a leader who will help others recognize that challenges are a part of life. We don't always get to choose our challenges, but we get to create the toolset to meet them. You can teach your team how to make the hard easier."

"Yes, I can!"

When Jabar met with his team, he started the meeting with a short self-introduction, and then he told them, "I am not here to make instant changes. I am not here to tell you our goals. The first thing I am here to do is to listen. I will schedule a meeting with each of you. What I want you to do is to have three questions that you want to ask me. I, in turn, will have questions to ask you. Then, we will decide together what needs to be changed, what needs to be emphasized, and what our goals will be."

Jabar made the hard easier by inviting discussion and creating a sense of unity at the very beginning of his new position. He quickly established a winning culture where the team learned the power of making the hard easier so that they increased their sales by 25% the first year and 40% the second year.

RELATE TO YOUR TEAM AT A DEEPER LEVEL

When we heal our wounds and grow ourselves to deeper levels, we develop better connections with our team members. When our team members understand how their emotions affect their ability to connect, we exhibit Olympic-level results.

Leaders who live according to the Winning Factors relate with their followers on a deeper level, creating a stronger bond with them. When I spoke with Carol Houle, SVP/Global Head of Financial Services and Insurance at Atos, she said that to solve business problems you must first build a connection with people. Carol said, "Everything that we do is about the customer and if it doesn't help the customer, we need to stop doing it."

The customer is both outside the organization and inside the organization. Each team member is considered a customer, and all actions and words are about building positive relationships. You've heard of the quote, "People only do business with those they know, like, and trust." This concept is not just for clients outside your organization; it is also for team members.

Winning Factor Leaders tend to have a greater understanding of themselves and their motivations, which heightens the capacity to empathize with others. Because people have a deep need to be understood, empathy is a link to knowing, liking, and trusting.

In college, Carol's quest for a closer relationship to God led her to a world religion class, which opened her mind to different possibilities beyond her Catholic upbringing. Carol spent time studying the Dalai Lama and time among monks in Sedona. Living in curiosity, she searched for the understanding of self within The Self. As her self-awareness grew, so did her capacity to understand and value others. She said, "Understanding people makes me feel closer to God. It helps me feel like I am doing God's work."

When leaders are not searching for validation, power, money, or titles, they are more present for their team members. Cultivating an environment where people feel supported and valued, Carol focuses on mentoring team members to reach their full potential.

Carol concentrates on what her team members are good at so that their passion about work increases. One of her favorite questions to ask team members is, *"What are the top three things that bring you energy?"* By discovering their expertise and passions, her team members are more likely to solve business problems, be engaged, and most importantly, love their jobs.

Winning Factor leaders place their ego in the backseat, focusing on giving rather than getting where the emphasis is about gifts to the world and celebrating as the people around them expand their talents. As a result of Carol's attention to purpose, positive energy, and connection, her team members often follow her from company to company.

Carol's leadership, with a deep emphasis on mindfulness, is not about religion. It is about self-awareness, compassion, love, joy, and happiness. Mindful leaders are not on a quest to alter their team member's religious beliefs, but rather to lead them to deeper peace through gaining wisdom. Greater peace could be in the form of practicing better communication skills, letting go of perfectionism, or recovering quickly from a mistake.

Mindful leadership comes from a place of tough love where we hold our team members to a higher level of accountability without judgment attached. Our goal is to allow them to find answers to the challenges that have long plagued them.

MAKE WORK ABOUT PURPOSE, IMPACT AND RELATIONSHIPS

The more we invest in our people, the more capacity they have for being present in their roles. One of those investments is to create unity among a diverse team, which means emphasizing the concept that ALL people are worthy. Division is often created when we see others as different from us rather than focusing on similar purposes that bring us together.

Ginny Chappell, EVP, Product and Marketing, of Moov Financial, and I spoke about the power of being authentic in your conversations and building bridges with your team. Early in her career, Ginny found that other professionals in her male-dominated field assumed that since she was a woman and pretty that she couldn't be smart and savvy. She determined that to be heard, she needed to make herself look as ugly as possible.

Fortunately, Ginny's early teachings from her Girl Scout leader, Margie Hershey, led her back to her roots of authenticity. Margie taught her Girl Scout Troop that they could be whatever they wanted to be if they lived their life with purpose and passion, true to themselves.

Ginny believes the key to relationships is to reveal to her team members that she is there to remove barriers for them.

Removing barriers requires a unique thought process for your team:

- Be curious about other people's hopes, dreams, and passions.

- Be open to disagreements while remaining focused on the team's values.

- Nobody can see through your head to your thoughts, so share your thoughts.

- Understand that people don't start their day saying, "I want to screw up today."

- Make certain that your expectations and rules of fair play are clear to others.

Ginny's philosophy is that work is a four-letter word. Most people work to get compensated, an obligatory commitment, but when we make it more about relationships, purpose, and impact, the more connected we are to our team members. People need to have both meaning and purpose, and the more we connect meaning and purpose with their roles, the more they love doing it, and the more they share the obstacles that prevent them from getting their jobs done.

The key to collaboration is to connect a diverse group of people with a common mission and purpose so that the team dynamic is magic. To do this, leaders must understand that our job is to make other people around us exceptionally brilliant. We cannot accomplish this unless we are aware that judging others by their physical attributes like Ginny's early peers did, is an act of organizational sabotage. People don't want to work at places where they feel that no matter what they do, it will never be good enough for the people around them.

THE WAY OF THE WINNING COMMUNICATOR

Collaboration is impossible without communication, and communication is impossible without the skillset to connect at an authentic level.

When I've asked audience members in my leadership seminars to describe a winning communicator, many people get confused about the differences between a forceful communicator and a winning communicator, because they rarely meet a person who practices winning conversations.

Winning communicators are confident and authentic. They actively listen, take in suggestions, acknowledge the value of other people's words, admit mistakes, respond rather than react, and stand firm in their decisions with the capacity to concede.

Because they are confident in who they are, they don't have to be right in a conversation, but they don't have to defer either. They offer solutions rather than dredging up complications. Wining communicators are in control of their emotions which allow them to think through their words before speaking, making them excellent leaders, parents, teachers, and team members because they value, respect, and hear others.

Below are three keys that are necessary for winning communicators:

1. **Self-awareness**: The capacity to recognize and control emotions before conveying them.

2. **Impulse control**: The ability to articulate emotions without utilizing bullying tactics.

3. **Self-confidence**: The skill to express beliefs without demeaning, judging, or demoralizing others.

Before and during conversations, winning communicators ask themselves three questions:

1. What is the outcome desired?

2. Did the other person feel heard?

3. Was my ego in charge?

TALKING IS THE GLUE THAT HOLDS RELATIONSHIPS TOGETHER

Through personal development and working on winning communication, our teams will possess the ability to respond rather than react. Thinking before speaking and speaking without intent to harm, converts into more beneficial conversations.

Changing another person is impossible but altering the way words are spoken allows others to hear each other better.

Without conversations, there are no relationships, and the more meaningful the conversation, the better the relationship. Valuable relationships are built on winning communication skills.

During my coaching career, I told my players daily, "Talking is the glue that holds the defense together." Our ability to communicate was the single most effective tool used to create a stifling defense. If a player forgot to call a screen, her teammate got blindsided, and our opponents scored.

Isn't this true about all communication—if we fail to have critical discussions, we get blindsided, and find ourselves on the losing end of the relationship?

Talking is the glue that holds relationships together.

The sad fact is that most people don't talk about vital issues, talking around concerns or avoiding them, hoping that the issues will get resolved without our participation.

Learning to respond rather than react, positively expressing emotions, standing up for beliefs without the need to right, and exuding confidence rather than cockiness is winning communication. Winning communicators find themselves in positions of leadership where people seek them for honest conversations and solutions, which brings wins to companies, teams, and organizations.

Our first response to disagreements is usually not collaboration. Our first response is the need to defend our thoughts, actions, ideas, methods, and beliefs. To get past our defense systems, we must have a strategy in place to direct the conversation. Failure to have a system, results in wasted energy and emotion.

The way to get beyond hours of internal fighting (i.e., justifying positions) is to keep the conversation moving forward rather than allowing for lengthy rationalizations and explanations which are often ego-based. A simple method for doing so is the ENAP Method:

E-Evidence: truth-only facts eliminating all subjective and descriptive language and emotions.

N-Narrative: history and relevant data to the current scenario.

A-Appraisal: the concerns, risks, and causes of the current situation and possible diagnostic tools and resources to move forward.

P-Proposals: the direction for successful resolution.

Having a system in place is the first step, but monitoring that system is essential to keep the ideas flowing forward. Discussion is important. Relaying the risks is also essential. How we present those ideas makes the progression faster and less confrontational.

While we want to raise concerns, we don't need to do so in such a fashion that irreparable harm occurs. Conflict is necessary as is expressing discontent. The methods we use to express our differences can either ignite or destroy a team.

During ENAP meetings, it is beneficial to have the following positions assigned to team members: parking lot attendant, timekeeper, and the referee. The parking lot attendant takes items that are important but not relevant to the current issue and places them in the parking lot. These items will be addressed at a later meeting or one-on-one discussion. In this way, the person has been heard and the meeting continues to flow on the topic at hand.

The timekeeper pushes the item forward if it has been exposed to the maximum and now repeats are the only narrative. The timekeeper can also move the topic forward from one person to another if one person is usurping all the time. "Thank you Mary for providing with those insights. Moving forward, Johnny would like to offer us his thoughts."

David Jacowitz, President of Evolution Financial Group, and I were discussing powerful meetings when he suggested using red flags and a referee. The red flag is thrown for personal fouls: side conversations, too many jokes, shifting topics, and finger-pointing. The foul results in a dollar contribution in a jar, and the money can later be distributed to the next meal, snacks, etc.

After employing the referee in a meeting, David said that it resulted in the most productive meeting his team had ever attended.

We are responsible for teaching our team members how to collaborate. While disagreements should be encouraged and discussions around differences promoted, we must teach our team how to have these disagreements in such a way that at the end of each meeting, progression toward a successful outcome has been reached. We are teachers, moderators, and facilitators supporting our teams to learn the best means of collaborating so that our team members continue to work together. We accept disputes but not disconnection from one another.

WINNING SUCCESS STEPS

1. List two ways you've been using a stick when you could have been using a bulldozer?
2. What are five ways you can build a team that collaborates with each other?
3. What are two ways you can relate to your team at a deeper level?

4. Blake Howitt said, "Your responsibility is to convince them of the truth about themselves that they don't yet understand." Write down three team members that are not working at their full potential. Now, what truth about themselves do they need to know? How can you best help them find that truth?

WINNING TAKEAWAYS

- The key is to make each person feel valued and the way to do that is to not be concerned about your level or their levels, but to see people as experts in their fields.
- "Your responsibility to your team is to convince them of the truth about themselves that they don't yet understand." Blake Howitt
- To get maximum results, we must be focused on building people rather than solely creating outcomes.
- The power in all relationships is to own your emotions, and to never allow any person to determine how you feel about you.
- Communication is not often received because emotions interfere with our ability to hear.
- People are ultimately responsible for who they become, but it is our responsibility to determine how or if their words will affect us.
- Leaders understand their job is to make other people around them exceptionally brilliant.
- When we teach our team members the keys to successful conversations rather than just expecting them to know how to converse, we provide them the opportunity for better relationships at work and at home.
- Talking is the glue that holds relationships together.

WINNING QUOTES:

"You can accomplish anything as long as the people on your team don't care who gets the credit."
Margaret O'Neal, CEO of United Way, WV

"In the midst of your career, find balance. Without balance, you will find emptiness."
Major General Jim Hoyer

"Get better at helping your team members become better."
Mark Geiselmayor, Director of Sales Channel-West, CCI Network Services

There are four traits that I govern my leadership by: 1) take less credit and give more; 2) establish a common purpose; 3) do the right thing; and 4) always be authentic."
Michael Frankel, SVP of Sales, North America at Selerant

"Just because you are a leader doesn't mean that you have everything fi figured out; that is why you have a team."
Michael Rider, Project Manager, Avitus Group

"You cannot just be results-focused where the only thing that counts is the goal. To get the best from your people, you must take time to understand them."
Mike Ross, President/CEO, CBS Banc-Corp and CB&S

"A difficult thing to accept and understand is that you can only change yourself. As you grow yourself, you have the power to influence others."
Pam Ferris, CEO of WV Leadership

"Part of the necessary growth of a leader is to understand how people perceive us."
Scott Coleman, COO of Fenice Community Media

"One of the greatest strengths of a leader is the ability to tell a story and get your team to buy into it."
Shari Krikorian, Payment Executive, Digital Transformation and Product Development, MasterCard (retired)

"You don't need to make tasks known to your team; you need to make them relevant."
Steve Bottfeld, CEO of Marketing Solutions, retired

"When communicating with other people, leave them a path out of the discussion at hand so that they don't feel compelled to dig in or act out."
Steve Torgeson, CTO, United Language Group

"We should share authentically and honestly about ourselves, not as a burden to others, but to share as humans."
Wesley Eugene, CIO, IDEO

"Invest in reverse mentoring. Think about what your team members can teach you."
Zachary Jones, President, First Market Bank

"Logic doesn't always matter; you've got to understand their perspective."
Adam Williams, CRO/VP, Private Equity

"Your energy and beliefs are transferrable to the people around you."
Ashwin Bharat, CEO of Revature

"When you think about leadership, you must think about legacy. How are you going to leave the organization a better place than when you came?"
Benita Fitzgerald, Olympian, Vice-President, LeagueApps

"Our job is to get people to recognize what they are good at and then play their strengths."
Charlie Johnson, SVP, Sales,
Payments Solutions & Digital Channels, Fiserv

"To create a great team, establish rules of engagement that are nonnegotiable in terms of how you work together and how you treat each other."
Cheryl Silverman, VP of IT,
First American Property and Casualty (retired)

"Match your will with a vision, and you are halfway to achieving whatever you want."
Donna DeVarona, Olympian, President at DAMAR Productions

"The highest level of engagement is allowing people to express their ideas even if it takes the conversation sideways. When you focus on ideas, great innovation takes place."
Harold Hughes, SVP of PNC

"My job is to hire good people, give them good training and resources, and then get out of their way."
Jason Hawkins, CEO of First United Bank, Kentucky

"The difference between a follower and a leader is perspective. Leaders understand they if they are not getting better, then neither are those around them."
Jeff Carroll, Former H.S. HOF Volleyball Coach,
Townsend Leadership Coach

"When dealing with other people, slow the movie down. Take time to pause, ponder, and then proceed."
John Fede, SVP, Technology, ENT Credit Union

"Manage your people by walking around, being present, asking questions, and being interested. If you want good results, you must inspect what you expect."
John Formica, Hotel Resort Leader,
Walt Disney Company (retired), Motivational Speaker

"Learn how to give and receive thorns and roses. Ask you, team members, to give you one thorn and two roses. A thorn is one thing you need to improve, and a rose is something you've done well. Then give them a thorn and two roses."
John Murray, Managing Director,
Research Circle Technology, GE Healthcare

"One of the most underused powers of leaders is storytelling. When you tell stories, you connect ideas and thoughts with people. Stories motivate, simplify, and engage your team members."
Karen Gilhooly, HSBC, Senior Executive Leader,
Financial Services and Global Transaction Banking

"Early in my career, I learned that some people didn't need me as their boss; what they needed from me was to have their backs."
Kelly Coleman, Owner and CEO of
Hancock Enterprises and P3Coleman Properties

"Culture is about you and me. It is about how we behave. It is not something out there; it is something we create together."
Krishna Bhakar, Founder/CEO of Ribon Gum Pvt. Ltd

"You don't have to hire the most qualified person, but you must hire the person who you most like to work with and who fits into your culture."
Lewis Keel, VP, Talent Solutions, Spring Point Technologies

"The biggest golden nuggets of leadership that I've learned are to know your people, make them feel valued, and show your appreciation to them."
Kyra Tehve Swallow, Chief of Staff, Banfield Pet Hospital

"When your team members don't see hope, it is hard for them to see opportunity."
Dr. Charcora Palmer, CEO, Total Power Financial Solutions LLC

"If money could solve the problem, is the solution really worth the money?"
Tim Stanley, President, Total Document Solutions

Chapter Six

Slash Excuses to Double Productivity

How many times have we listened to excuses when our team members failed to meet a deadline or turned in less than stellar work?

How we handle excuse-making determines a high-performance or low-performance team.

Acknowledge that excuse-making is the nature of people because excuses enable them to feel better about failing. Blaming other people or circumstances lifts the burden of guilt. This mind trick overcomes the notion that they are not good enough to succeed, but it prevents progress. The feel-good emotion of "not my fault" is short-lived because nothing has changed in terms of accomplishment.

Instead of permitting team members to use excuses and point fingers, teach them the power of failing fast and pivoting to solutions. *When 100% responsibility for failures is assumed and excuses are banned, success is more easily attained.*

Benji Bruce, a multi-millionaire, one of my mentors, and owner of Speaker's Academy, said, "If something is not working, it is because you are not doing it right. Even if you are doing the right things, you might not be doing them the right way."

To effectively pivot, teach your team that *failure is not fatal but that making excuses for failing is the fatality.* Reinforce that beating themselves up or placing blame is the opposite of success and leads to self-doubt. Self-doubt leads to procrastination, apathy, and grief.

Because our team members are the lifeblood of our success, we don't accept them as they are; we push them beyond their current self-defined limitations.

Coach your team to recognize that self-doubt in the form of excuses is a wake-up call to learn more. When their actions are failing, they are unaware of the right path. There is no need for debasement or demoralization because that is a waste of time and energy. Beating them up does not make them better, nor does it resolve the issue.

Be aware of the top excuses that people use. Guard your team against these excuses, and if they make one of them, have them pivot to self-responsibility and knowledge.

Below is a list of the top nine excuses people use:

- I'm overtasked and overburdened.

- That's not my responsibility.

- I'll come back to it later.

- I don't have all the pieces to the equation yet.

- I need the boss to tell me exactly what to do.

- I don't understand how I am going to get this done.

- I don't see the reward for me.

- I might not get the recognition I deserve.

- My quality of work might not be good enough.

- I might flop, bomb, or totally disappoint.

While leaders are challenged by balancing micro-managing with accountability, we must find the pathway to holding people answerable for doing their jobs. We must know the difference between what a fact is and what is a justification for not getting a job done.

We must be aware that excuses are easier than ownership, and that what we let slide becomes the norm.

If our teams are laden with excuses, it is because they don't understand the power of taking 100% responsibility for their actions. While it is time consuming to address excuses, it is far more damaging to our team morale, productivity, and goals if excuses are tolerated.

Below are five ways to eliminate excuses from the workday.

- Align with your choices.

- Amplify accountability.

- Emphasize the next steps.

- Boost their inner winners.

- Focus on the winning ways.

THE BEST ACTION ARISES FROM BETTER CHOICES

When we teach the power of choices, we enable our team members to be in control of their lives. Our team members may not like the choices in front of them, but there is an option that will lead to less discomfort. They might feel that choices are burdensome because they lead to experiences which, in turn, lead to consequences.

The choice in front of our team members may not be as burdensome as their imagination causes it to seem. It is their imagination about harmful consequences that impair them the most. We often imagine negative outcomes about an upcoming event. For example, there is a toxic person on the team that others avoid like the coronavirus, and this individual is also one of the best salespeople on the team.

Because we fear the outcome of terminating this person, we create a story around what will happen when he is fired. The story might go like this: if we let this salesperson go, then they will be hired by our number one competitor and then our competitor will blow us away in sales.

The story is just a story. It has no facts based on it except that it was created through fear.

The stories we create through fear don't feel good.

The greater a burden is perceived in a task; the more excuses are likely to be formed. In other words, *we make excuses when acting feels hard.* We have a choice to either keep the employee or terminate him. Because the choice feels difficult, we fail to act.

We've allowed decisions to hinder our actions which causes us to get caught up in details like *when* is the best time to terminate or *how* can I terminate the individual? Once those questions enter our minds, we are more likely to dive into rationales about how firing the employee will wreak havoc on achieving our goals. *As a result of our rationales, which are just excuses dressed up in formal attire, the hard questions continue to be concealed while our culture suffers.*

The more complex a situation is, the more we must divide it into parts. In this situation, rather than focusing on the how and the when, focus on the why and the what. Why should we take this action? What is the right action to take? By focusing on the why and the what, the justification for not acting dwindles.

AMPLIFY ACCOUNTABILITY

One way to create accountability and avoid excuses is to use a blueprint. A blueprint provides a clear set of guidelines for the responsibilities of team members and the means for measuring their progress. This way, everyone knows where they stand and there is less room for ambiguity or misinterpretation.

Not everyone is going to be happy with this type of system. Some people may feel like they don't have enough freedom within the confines of the framework. The key is that everyone—not just the leaders—knows what is expected of them and their roles and responsibilities, which means there are no excuses. Period.

When I interviewed Nandini Srinivasan, VP of Quality Assurance at Motive, it took me two seconds to recognize a voice of accountability. She exuded the confidence of a commander where her expectations were clear on what needed to be done, how it needed to be done, and when it was due.

Nandini learned accountability through her father and grandfather's questioning at the dinner table. She is a native of India where she was educated at a Catholic Convent. Her father and grandfather were both literary geniuses and loved the classics. Their dinner conversations were centered around the thirty-seven literary works of Shakespeare. Her father and grandfather peppered her and her siblings with questions about Shakespeare's thirty-seven works expecting them to answer intelligently. This was Nandini's first understanding of how preparation and knowledge led to positive reinforcement.

When Nandini moved to the United States, she was fortunate that her first leader was a great mentor who taught her the key to accountability which was that she was not responsible for other people's lack of planning.

Nandini learned that leaders who hold people accountable don't concern themselves with seeking the title of Ms. Congeniality. In fact, accountable leaders are often seen as unwanted guests because they ask difficult questions. To be the person who can ask penetrating questions, Nandini said that you must invest in personal relationships and create trust so that your team members recognize that you are not being adversarial. Tough questions lead to quality work and job security.

Accountability builds trust and cooperation among team members because the pathway to success is clear, leaving no room for finger pointing. The three steps below are necessary for running a blueprint once it is established and for keeping team members moving positively toward successful outcomes.

1
Trust in the capabilities of your team.

When we trust in our team members, they feel confident in their role within the team which makes them more likely to collaborate effectively and contribute to the success of the team. Additionally, when team members feel trusted and supported by their leaders and colleagues, they are more likely to feel fulfilled and motivated in their work. Trust within a team adds to increased innovation, because team members feel more comfortable sharing ideas and taking risks.

When employees know they can count on us to hold them accountable, it eliminates excuses, builds trust that all team members are doing their part, and makes people more likely to do their best work. This simple principle is one that can be easily implemented in our workplace by setting clear expectations from the top down. Make it a habit to provide positive reinforcement and constructive feedback—both of which help improve performance. When employees know they are valued and respected, eliminating excuses becomes much easier.

2
Share the purpose behind each task.

There are always reasons to do something, but sometimes it's hard to find the right ones. When we ask team members to do something, they need to know why the task is important and why it needs to be done in the timeline indicated. This helps them see the task in a new light and eliminates any excuses they might have. It also makes them more likely to take on the challenge, knowing that it matters both to us and the organization.

There is a reason why it's important to eliminate excuses at work. When we allow reasons for not getting something done, we make it seem less important. Injecting personal stakes into the situation assures our team members what we're asking is worth their time and effort. By making our requests clear and putting ourselves in the shoes of those we're asking, we can help ensure that they see the importance of our request and are more likely to take it on.

3
Follow-up regularly.

Eliminating excuses at work can be a difficult task, but it is important to set clear expectations with team members and check in on their progress regularly. Checking in not only reinforces the importance of the work, but also our expectations that team members will achieve the agreed-upon goals. Checking in reassures our team that we are watching and available to them. This reinforces their need to be responsible and gives them a sense of ownership over their work.

When we manage by walking around, checking in, and asking questions, our team members know that we care. They also recognize that we will not tolerate laziness or poor work ethic. While some people might get irritated by our thoroughness, our top performers will love us and be motivated to accomplish even more work.

ACCOUNTABILITY IS A NECESSARY COMPONENT OF ALL SUCCESS

Nadya Rousseau learned as a young woman that accountability for her actions led to greater results. She is now a valued friend who I gained during the process of interviewing her and is the founder of Alter New Media, a marketing and media company.

Nadya graduated as a junior from high school at the age seventeen, skipping her senior year. That summer she took a trip to California to meet Lauren, nineteen, who she had been conversing with online for a year. The following summer, Nadya moved to California to be with Lauren. After floundering for five months in California, close to homelessness, Nadya and Lauren moved back to Maryland and in with Nadya's parents. After two days of returning to Maryland, Nadya's mother demanded that she get a job.

Nadya understood that nobody was going to save her; she needed to save herself, so she took two jobs to make money—one as a floor supervisor at Izod and another one at the Kitchen Collection. After three months working two jobs, she gained a job at Citigroup in the retention department. After saving money for nine months, Nadya and Lauren moved back to California where they remained for fourteen years. During those years, Nadya acted, hosted, and produced a television show.

Both Lauren and Nadya began dabbling in social media in 2012. In 2016, Nadya was working part-time at a law firm as a paralegal and legal collector, studying as a university student, producing a television show, and building a client base for her new digital media marketing agency. By January 2017, she was full time at her new company, bringing her partner, Lauren, in as co-founder in 2018.

Aside from Lauren, her wife, the team is 100% remote. Though Nadya ultimately departed her university studies to pursue her business full-time, she continued her education through trial and error, masterminds, reading, studying and asking questions. Her curiosity and willingness to grow have contributed to the growing success of Alter New Media.

With a remote group of team members, the duo has learned to rely on project management systems to communicate with their team members. They also communicate via Slack so that their team members have immediate access to them, and they have immediate access to their team members.

To maintain accountability, each team member is connected to a standard operating procedures manual, and when they are onboarded, they learn brand strategy, values, mission statements, and the vision of Alter New Media. Nadya holds regular trainings to make certain that her team members know and understand their processes.

Nadya and Lauren's challenges are like most of our challenges--allowing their team members to work autonomously while keeping a system of accountability. This is where we as leaders are challenged to become coaches. A coach sets the following structure:

C-Collective goals.

O-Obvious expectations.

A-Alignment through critical (winning) conversations.

C-Coach by asking great questions.

H-Have clear consequences for missing deadlines, not following procedures, and poor behaviors.

As Nadya and Lauren have continued to grow their company, they've learned that building accountability is necessary for building trust among team members, creating positive relationships, and minimizing costly mistakes. Nadya had to learn as a young adult to be accountable for her outcomes, not looking for anybody else to save her. What she learned as a leader is that not everybody was like her; her team members needed accountability and training by somebody outside of themselves. Lauren and Nadya continue to find ways to coach their team members so that accountability is a welcomed expectation that provides all of them with the greatest possibility of success.

EMPHASIZE THE NEXT STEPS

Eliminating excuses is a key part of keeping our team's focus on the next action. By focusing on what needs to be done and not what might go wrong, our team members can move forward with confidence. This mindset enables our teams to achieve goals faster and with less stress.

People often make excuses for why they cannot complete a task or meet a deadline. This can be due to a lack of understanding or knowledge of the task at hand, personal circumstances outside of work, or simply feeling overwhelmed. Often, these excuses are deployed as a shield to justify inaction and/or lack of results.

To combat this problem, make certain that team members are well-informed about the task at hand and provide clear instructions and deadlines. Additionally, encourage team members to seek support from their colleagues when needed and report any problems they encounter. By doing so, we can help eliminate the excuses that often stand in the way of success at work.

The goal of eliminating excuses at work is to remove the barriers that excuse-makers use to avoid acting. Here are three steps to eliminate excuses from team members:

1. Understand the reasons why excuse-makers might make a particular excuse. Often, there is a hidden agenda behind an excuse that goes beyond simply solving the problem at hand. For example, excuse-makers might be afraid of criticism or confrontation, or they may feel threatened by someone else on the team. Understanding why individuals are making excuses will help us better manage them and get them on board with our plans.

2. Eliminate any potential distractions from the task at hand. If we are requiring individuals to complete a project, be sure that they are not being distracted by other tasks or concerns in their life. If there are any distractions present, clear them away so the individuals can focus on what needs to be done.

3. Teach our teams to be prepared for obstacles along the way and their resistance to those obstacles. Obstacles are a certainty with any project. It is not the obstacle that prevents people from working; it is their resistance to the obstacle.

Here is a three-step process to support team members in moving beyond challenges. Ask them:

- What are the controllable factors? From those factors, what steps can be taken right now?

- Imagine another solution. What does that solution look like?

- What is one way to shift the obstacle in front of you?

When our team members have clarity around the three-step process, have them write down immediate steps they can take today to move forward and a deadline for completion of the project.

BOOST THEIR INNER WINNERS

Many excuses are born from uncertainty.

> *When we don't believe in ourselves, it is easy to create what we think are concrete reasons why something cannot be achieved.*

We are likely to claim that our bosses, leaders, parents, or spouses don't believe in us; therefore, we won't be able to achieve our desires.

I've had dozens of conversations with players who came to my office asking me to give them confidence. The conversation would go something like this:

"Coach, I need you to believe in me so that I can play better."

My response was, "If you want me to believe in you, then you must first believe in yourself."

"But if you don't think I can be a great player, then I will never be that player."

I understood their line of thinking because I had been imprisoned by that excuse. During the seven and a half years I played for the USA National Team Handball Team, I ached for my coach to validate his belief in me. I believed his confidence would make me a better player. My thought process failed me in three ways:

1. I had no control over my coach's ability to understand psychology, spirituality, or people.

2. I gave him dominion over my confidence.

3. I never achieved my potential waiting for him to tell me that I was good.

As a result, I allowed my coaches to determine how I played, which was far below my abilities. From my experiences as a player, I knew that my athletes needed to understand their power.

I told my players. "I understand that you believe I need to tell you how great you are, and I've already told you that. I recruited you because you are great. It doesn't matter how many times I tell you that you are awesome if you don't believe it. I'm here to guide your greatness, to help you unravel your full potential, but I can't provide you with confidence. *Your job is to know how great you are. My job is to assure you that you are correct.*"

Your team members might believe, like many of my former players, that to succeed other people must believe in them.

If people use the excuse that they don't have enough support, understand they suffer from a lack of belief in their inner winners. An essential teaching point for teams is: Nobody can connect them with their inner winners. Their responsibility is to know that they were born winners, because we were all born as winners. While we can express confidence in them, they must hear it and allow themselves to align with their values.

This is the ultimate catch-22. Before anybody can see our true greatness, we must know our greatness. When we are in alignment with our greatness, then everybody recognizes our greatness.

While we don't have the ability to connect other people with their inner winners, we can lead them toward the pathway of self-empowerment. Because they don't know what they don't know, ask them questions which support self-awareness.

Below are key teaching questions to ask for self-reflection:

- Will you regret your decision ten years from today if you fail to reach your full potential because you allowed another person's opinion to stop you?

- When searching for other people's words to validate you, will their words **ever live up to your needs**?

- Does living in the limitation of your potential feel good?

- How does living in the expansion of your talents feel different than limiting your talents?

- Do you want other people *granted access to your personal power when their ideas about you might be completely unjustified, senseless, or unsubstantiated?*

- Do you want to waste your time on another person's opinions about you when they **can't understand or acknowledge** the views that they have about **themselves**?

- When other people blast dissenting opinions about your goals and ideas, does that mean you are on the wrong path or *that they can't visualize your path?*

When we encounter people who fail to believe in us, we have three choices:

- Number one: Explain our beliefs to them so that they can see what we know.

- Number two: Share our plans for forward progression so they understand our passions.

- Number three: Ignore them so they don't deter us from our greatness.

Other people cannot understand what is possible or impossible for us because they view us from their winner killers—the places where they can't see their possibilities. Therefore, I prefer method number three. It doesn't matter if anybody else believes in us or has the same vision as we do. What matters is the belief we have in ourselves.

Period.

When our teams understand the CATCH-22 and grasp that they are born as winners and all they must do is eradicate the voices of people who are winner killers, then excuses don't need to be made about OTHER people not giving them what they need. They will find a way.

GAIN BACK YOUR DREAMS THROUGH WINNING AWARENESS

In 2019, I flew to Alabama to speak to a crowd of 5,000 at the Alabama State SHRM (Society for Human Resources) Conference. After I had finished speaking, an audience member asked if I had time to speak with her.

"I would love to. What is on your mind?"

Jada said, "During your speech you said that to experience success we had to take 100% responsibility for our lives, but I can't have financial freedom because it is my responsibility to take care of my family. I can't have what I want, because I must first give to my mother, son, and daughter." *(I can't have is another form of an excuse.)*

Jada continued, "My mother and grandmother taught me that service to others is my duty. Other people should come before my needs, so I must give to others before I give to myself."

"How old are your children?'

Jada responded, "They are 29 and 30. Both live at home. I am supporting them as they work so that they can save money to buy their houses. And my mother also lives with me because she hates living alone."

"Do any of them pay for rent or food? Do they do some service for you in return for your goodwill?"

Jada blew out a deep breath. "No. They live off of me."

I asked, "How do you feel when your surrender your dreams to make other people feel better?"

"Angry."

"Did you ever consider that you are hurting the people around you by giving too much and depriving them the responsibility of caring for themselves?"

Jada widened her eyes, "What?"

"How does it hurt other people when you don't allow them the experience of learning to take care of themselves?"

Jada exclaimed, "Oh my gosh! I've been hurting my children by giving them too much! AND…hurting myself in the process. You've just given me permission to care for myself."

"Yes, and be free of guilt, which allows you to give freely. When you give now, you won't feel as if you *should* give, and you won't have the excuse that you can't have financial freedom."

Wiping tears from her eyes, Jada replied, "Yes. I see that now. I don't have to give. When I give when I don't want to give but feel like I should, I'm angry. I've been denying myself time and energy through the excuse that I had to give to others first. But, when I give from a full slate after giving to myself, I will love giving again. I just gained ten years in my life, because you freed me from the *shoulds*. I don't need to support them; they need to support themselves."

"Yes, *and when you support yourself more and stop searching for self-worth through giving to others, you will be free to love yourself more and give from love, which will feel totally different.*"

"Hmm…let me think on that one. What you are saying is that I am looking for my self-worth through them? That is why it makes me angry to give?"

"Yes."

"But I am a giving person. I don't need to give to other people to make me feel good."

"Okay."

Jada turned to walk away, stopped, and came back to me. "You said okay, but I sense you believe that I am wrong."

"No. You are not wrong. This is your journey to self-awareness. Not mine. Just sit with that statement and feel it. If you object too strongly to the words, then own them. If you don't object too strongly, then they weren't true."

Jada stood silently for a minute and then said, "I protested too much."

I answered with a smile.

Jada, like many of us, failed to understand that we search for validation in a myriad of ways. When other people don't give us what we need in the ways that we need it, anger becomes a mainstay in our lives. We've given our power away, and it is always our responsibility to keep our power.

When we use excuses to validate why we do what we do or can't obtain what we want, and anger becomes a mainstay in our lives, we've cut ourselves off from the awareness that the **only person who can validate us enough is us**. Self-support is not selfish; it is critical to our ability to expand.

Champions of life accept responsibility and ask others to do the same. In this way, all of us can find freedom to achieve more.

FOCUS ON YOUR HEART-WIN

All excuses are dipped in fear. *Not one excuse we make is in alignment with brave beliefs, because brave beliefs are the essence of expansion*. Fear is the essence of smallness. Connecting to our heart-wins (the deep, driving purpose that surpasses all need to doubt) drives alignment with our goals.

When our team members question how they will be able to accomplish a task, they are afraid of their inability to complete the goal. Behind their fear is a not-good-enough belief disguised as the reason the goal is unattainable.

At the beginning of a project or goal, all the answers are not available to us. We can plan and strategize, but there will be challenges that change the course of our actions.

If we cannot begin a project until we have the outcome clearly known, then we will never begin the process.

If the road map for success was known, we would follow it. Because we cannot predict the future, the first question that comes to mind is, "How will I achieve this goal?" What stops us from acting is fear of the unknown and the need to know how the goal will be achieved.

Once the question of how something will get accomplished gets into the minds of our team members, fear is in control, separating them from their heart-wins. The how question spins them into stalemate because when they question, faith in themselves is minimalized causing them to delay and avoid action.

One of my coaching clients, "Debbie," wanted to create a small business, but she had no business background. Whenever we shared a coaching call, she explained to me that she didn't know how to get her business running profitably. She assured me that if she just knew how to grow her business that she would take the appropriate steps.

I said, "Debbie, if you separate yourself from action by remaining in the fuzziness of how it will occur, you will never move from where you are. The most important thing that you can do is focus on connecting with what makes your heart happy, what I call a heart-win. Why do you want this business to be profitable? What will profit give you? And why is that important to you? What does it feel like to have the things you desire?"

The ego wants us to remain in safety mode by asking how each step is going to evolve. When we are creative, innovative, and expanding, our alignment is with our heart wins. Questioning how a goal will occur prevents action while stepping into the feeling that makes our hearts happy, a heart-win, creates an emotion connected to a positive outcome.

When we are connected to a deep passion or an outcome, then our inspiration overrides the fear of how our goals will get accomplished. The emotion of fear, often disguised as safety or survival, keeps us static.

Take a moment to ask your team members how. How will they become a marathon runner? How will they make a million dollars? How will they become CEO of a Fortune 500 company? How will they find the perfect partner? How will they get healthy? How will they build a successful business?

After asking those questions, ask them if they felt fear or brave beliefs. There might be a mixture of answers, but if they are self-aware, they will know that diving deeper into winning the outcome of each goal creates fear.

Change their focus from fear to a heart-win. What will achieving that goal give them? If they cannot find a big enough heart win that stirs them to action, they will always be deadlocked in the wanting of something but not believing they can achieve it.

Debbie let go of questioning how when she focused on her biggest heart win—the freedom to work when and how she desired, which allowed her to spend more time with her children. Once her focused shifted, Debbie acted consistently toward her dream leading her to own a profitable t-shirt business within six months.

Switch off the question of how the goal will happen, because this is a form of worry, which creates anxiety, which does nothing but consume time. Focus instead on heart-wins, the passion connected to the goal, and use imagination to fuel action. Imagination of the positive outcome along with a deep reason for the goal propels action.

Inaction is tied to the belief that dreams are illusions, which is why getting stuck on how it will happen is a dream-killer.

If we must focus on the how, change the question to align with the outcome.

- How will the feeling of satisfaction flow through you?

- How will the accomplishment of your goal positively impact others?

- How will your goal look when completed?

- How will your sense of achievement inspire you toward your next goal?

- How will you and your loved ones celebrate?

The focus of our minds is the answer. Questioning how can be a positive if used in terms of expressing the feelings of success or detrimental when combined with the concept of the unknown.

SHIFTING YOUR TEAM'S EXCUSES TO POWERFUL SOLUTIONS

Reasons are excuses dressed up in tuxedos, but even dressed up, excuses are still limitations. They hold us back, let us down, and prevent hope. Releasing excuses and holding ourselves accountable for everything is powerful because we are the answer.

One of the most potent things we can do as leaders is to shift from giving feedback to asking questions which promote self-awareness. Telling others what to do rarely results in behavioral changes. Asking questions dives directly into empowering others to see what actions they can take to create better outcomes.

Teaching ourselves to recognize excuses is the first step. The second step is to hold people accountable for their excuses. The third step is to promote further growth through self-awareness. We cannot help others to help themselves if they don't see the problem as themselves.

WINNING SUCCESS STEPS

1. What are two excuses you've allowed your team to make that if you hadn't allowed the excuses, you would have doubled productivity?
2. What are two ways you can shift the fear around challenging goals, so the focus is on the positive outcome?
3. What are two key questions you can ask which enables your team members to connect with their inner winners?

Winning Takeaways

- When 100% responsibility for failures is assumed and excuses are banned, success is more easily attained.
- To effectively pivot, teach your team that failure is not fatal but that making excuses for failing is the fatality.
- We must be aware that excuses are easier than ownership, and that what we let slide becomes the norm.
- As a result of our rationales, which are just excuses dressed up in formal attire, the hard questions continue to be concealed while our culture suffers.
- When we don't believe in ourselves, it is easy to hold onto what we think are concrete reasons why something cannot be achieved.
- Do you want other people granted access to your personal power when their ideas about you might be

- completely unjustified, senseless, or unsubstantial-ted?
- When other people blast dissenting opinions about your goals and ideas, does that mean you are on the wrong path or that they can't visualize your path?
- Self-support is not selfish; it is critical to our ability to expand.
- Not one excuse we make is in alignment with brave beliefs, because brave beliefs are the essence of expansion.

Winning Quotes

"Don't take anybody's advice for face value. Listen. Take what is meaningful for your experience and let the rest go."
Prasad Rani, VP, Data Governance Manager, TCW

"Understand what behaviors you need to engage in to get the results you want."
Dr. Paul Gavoni, COO BDI Media

Teach people that the words 'I can't ' do not live within your organization."
Randie Lawson, CEO, Mountain State Waste Company

"We were conditioned to ask permission to become great. We forget that we already have the power within us. We don't need approval from anybody except ourselves."
Rodney Walker, President of Grant Central USA

"Remember that 'the who' matters.
We must listen, understand personalities,
and know our teams to drive success."
Souheil Badran, EVP, COO, Northwestern Mutual

"The dialogue in our heads is either a blessing or a curse. We
must pay attention to how to make the dialogue a blessing."
Till Paris, CEO, Dream Team Media

"Knowledge paired with understanding gives you wisdom, and
the most essential thing a leader can do is to transfer that
wisdom to others."
Tuff Harris, CEO of One Heart Warrior

"Leaders must have the capacity to win people to a common
understanding."
Alan Rogers, Chair, Board of Advisors,
Center of Leadership, UC-Boulder

"Continue to work on yourself. Be open to new areas of
growth and encourage others to do the same."
Andrew Newman, Owner at Newman Restoration & Cleaning

"Fire fast and hire slow. Hire the people that fit into your
culture and that work at the level of your team."
Bob Steensma, CEO of Five Star Credit Union

"Realize that working people out of a business or firing people
is often in their best interest."
Dave Laux, GM and VP, Lumen Technologies

"To be a great CEO, you must learn to make unpopular decisions and worry less about making people happy and more about the right decisions for the company."
Eric Schreimann, CEO, Club Fitness

"Convince the people around you that to reach a goal that everybody has to get in the boat, pick up an oar, and row together."
Jim Leahy, CEO of USA Luge, Retired

"Leadership is the ability to be in alignment with your integrity so that you can have the conversations around integrity with your team members and call them out if necessary."
Judy Casperson, VP, Key Bank

"The key to growth is taking feedback from your customers, articulate what they need and build it quickly."
Madhu Bala, VP, SBU Head

"Always be curious. Ask questions. Ask why after the ask. Then look at the result and ask is it the one we want?"
**Max Baucus, U.S. Senator 1978-2014,
longest serving senator from Montana**

"If you are the smartest person in your circle, get a new circle."
Michael Lewis, Area Manager, NurseCore

"It is okay to fail. In fact, it is necessary. Make failing opportunities into something positive."
**Mitze Amorosco, SVP, CIO,
Director of Information Services, ArchCare**

"Leadership is about the big picture; you cannot get bogged down in the small details or you will never move forward."
Neil Greer, CEO and Co-Founder of Impact Engine

"Make it super easy for people to give you feedback and then act on their feedback."
Patrick Byrne, CEO, GE Renewable Energy Onshore Wind

"Business is all about relationships—the ability to interact and engage and to guide or be guided."
Joan Quintana, Managing Director, AdventGX

"Success is a psychological battle. Develop habits to keep you fueled and ready to battle."
Jason Knickerbocker, Owner Tax Scout, Co-Founder of BeWizeApp

"Successful teams are created through accountability and having tough conversations. When people know what is expected and you hold them accountable to expectations, most of them succeed."
Mary D. Madden, President/CEO, Hudson Valley Credit Union

Chapter Seven

Creating the Multiplier Effect

As leaders, we can allow our team members to settle in, kick back, put their feet up, and glide through life on what they know...or we can give them greater tools so that they can choose the experience that will multiply their happiness, goals, and life experiences. While some people think that they are happy when they are settled into the relative safety of a comfort zone, those same folks have accepted they will never win all their goals, life is full of hardships, and winning at the highest level is outside their reach.

Most people settle into those beliefs because they experienced a loss or a failure. They've allowed past experiences to define current situations. They don't want to expand because expansion is a risk and with risk, there is the potential for injury.

As leaders, we have the capacity to provide the multiplier effect where people gain new insights that allow for greater growth. They don't have to settle for a life less than full when we have the capacity to coach them to think differently.

Through team meetings, lunch and learns, book clubs, and outside experts, we can show our team members a new way of thinking that expands their abilities.

One of the superpowers we own is that we can create a ripple effect which moves from the workspace into our homes and communities. We can create a better world one team member at time with the knowledge that what we teach can multiply tenfold.

> *Productivity is always the result of what we think, and if we think we are at full capacity, then we are stuck living the life we've created in our minds.*

The greatest joys of most of the leaders I spoke with was the success of their team members moving beyond self-imposed limitations. When I asked the interviewees what their biggest success was, over 95% of them responded how their team overcame a great obstacle or how some of their team members became C-Suite executives.

We can do great good in this world by supporting our team members in such a fashion they attain a winning attitude.

We can re-teach and eliminate some of the concepts that have handcuffed them to their present state of being. While not every team member will receive our gifts, because they are not ready to receive them, those who accept our knowledge and wisdom will evolve mentally, emotionally, and spiritually. They become the multipliers of all the lessons we've learned.

I've offered six chapters in this book chocked full of WINNING information guaranteed to help you win as a leader, and this chapter is the most powerful, because what we do with the information is far more important than knowing it.

When I was in college, my basketball coach, Bud, had a wealth of basketball knowledge, which he never shared with his team. He would drive four hours to scout an opponent, get home at three in the morning with his notebook full of information and never give it to us. I couldn't understand why he would go to all that trouble to learn information that could get us a victory and not give it to us.

- Did he think we weren't smart enough to understand the scouting reports?

- Did he believe that only he needed the knowledge?
- Did he imagine by giving his knowledge away that he would no longer be needed?

I believed as a player if I had the information that Bud knew, I would have been a better player, and therefore, would have made him a better coach. But Bud never shared, and I was left playing with what I knew.

When I became a college coach, I resolved that ALL my players would be as smart if not smarter than I was. I would teach them the game like they were all coaches. Not only would I offer them the X's and O's of the game, but I would also give them the winning attitude needed to be victorious on the court and in life.

What I discovered was that we won more games because the players were smart enough to adjust on their own. They were smarter than their opponents and this gave them a mental advantage, and yes, sometimes they were smarter than me which resulted in more wins for the team.

Teach your team everything you know, then learn more and teach them more. Give them the reins to make decisions, to be innovative, and to provide insights. Give them the toolset so that the cycle of student and teacher becomes the same. The teacher can learn from the student and the student from the teacher. In this way, you are ever-expanding.

The X's and O's of any organization begins and ends with people, which means it is essential to create the winning attitude that creates the multiplier effect:

- Find your victory formula.

- Build your team's mental toughness.

- Leverage the winner's focus.

- Stop the chaos.

- Be an appreciation magnet.

- Live in the success zone.

- Be curious.

FIND YOUR VICTORY FORMULA

Being stagnant in a vibrant world where nothing remains the same except change itself is a formula for calamity.

If we cannot adapt, we will not succeed.

Everything in our universe is in a constant state of transition, and if we are in a constant state of sameness, then the world moves on without us, and we cannot serve the people around us who are elevating their Winning Factors.

While some people are addicted to being stuck, Kathy Chou, one of the brilliant leaders I interviewed, is not one of them.

Kathy Chou, SVP of SaaS Engineering at Nutanix, is a Stanford Medal Recipient, one of the top 100 most influential women named by Silicon Valley Business Journal, and a real down-to-earth mother of four boys.

Kathy is brilliant, empathetic, easy-going, friendly, and self-aware. We were five minutes into our interview when Kathy exposed her courage by being vulnerable, sharing her story about how her biggest challenge was building confidence.

Growing up, her father, Philip Ko, often told her that she could be or do anything. He repeated the tale about shooting high to Kathy hundreds of times.

- If you shoot high, you might get the middle.

- If you shoot for the middle, you might get the low.

- If you shoot low, you get nothing.

Despite his belief in her, Kathy was shy and introverted, often eating her lunch alone in the girl's locker room. Coping from a lack of confidence, Kathy turned to perfectionism. In 5th grade, her teacher instructed the class that they had to write a one-page paper in pen without a single mistake. Kathy wrote that paper 40 times to comply with her teacher's request. Because she was afraid to make a mistake, she worked harder and harder to know the answers, which became a problem within itself.

Because perfectionists are harder on themselves than anybody else, they beat themselves up when they fail to live up to their standards. This behavior perpetuates the very thing they are trying to escape-not being good enough.

Kathy's father continued to share his belief in her, prodding her to be the best version of herself. In 8th grade during the awards ceremony at the end of the year, Kathy won the top academic award for every single subject. The awards provided her confidence in the world of academics but didn't change her lack of self-assurance in anything else.

Philip Ko, worried about his daughter's lack of socialization skills, signed her up for Junior Achievement. In Junior Achievement, Kathy met people who led her through her comfort zone to bigger accomplishments. She took a Dale Carnegie course and learned entrepreneurial skills. As her self-awareness grew, Kathy knew that she needed to surrender the parts of her which didn't support her like the nickname her schoolmates gave her: "The Walking Brain." Kathy knew that defining herself as a single element would not empower her, so she went out for cheerleading and track.

In each phase of her life, Kathy altered or surrendered the self-defined restrictions that no longer served her. She learned to embrace her intelligence while accepting that she was beyond a walking brain. She became more social, surrendering her shyness. She renounced the need to have all the answers so that she could empower herself to ask questions and learn from others.

If we exert too much time and energy bonding with things, people, ideas, concepts, self-definitions, and emotions, our lives become exploited with trivial things that don't serve us well.

Those trivial things that we see as essential take up residency in our minds which become too full to allow for better opportunities.

When we consciously renounce the thoughts that no longer serve us, our minds will be filled with the freedom to choose how we want to show up in life. When we are taxed emotionally, physically, mentally, or spiritually, we have the capacity to drop our attachment to those thoughts providing ourselves with a clean slate to create something even better.

Kathy discarded the pieces of her that no longer served her so that she increased her capacity to lead herself, her family, and her team. Through the process of surrendering old definitions, Kathy found the keys to coaching her team members so that they are not stuck in a silo, a problem, or even their narrow self-definitions.

BUILD YOUR TEAM'S MENTAL TOUGHNESS

During the 12 years that I trained twice a day for the Olympics, I understood that physically training my body would enhance my chances of making the USA Team. Every Olympic athlete that I knew believed in training their bodies so that their skills would provide them with increased confidence, improved concentration, and better opportunities for victory.

Training your body was essential for making the Olympic team, but training your mind was the difference between being an average or a great Olympian. Our coaches didn't believe in training the mind and were afraid of sports psychologists, because they thought that an outside expert would ruin our thinking.

My Russian coach, Ilya, told me, "You don't need to think. I know more and think more. You know nothing. Don't think." If I could have turned off my thinking—the self-doubts, the fear of not being good enough, the questions in my mind about whether to shoot or not, I would have been three times as good...and I would have not listened to voice of my coaches who didn't know how to provide positive feedback. They were confidence crushers.

After a game where I scored seven goals, which is a phenomenal accomplishment in the sport of European handball, my coach pulled me aside. "Sherry, Why you do this—shoot nine times and score seven goals? You are not a goal scorer. You are playmaker. Make plays. Don't shoot."

Even though I understood I helped us win the game and that my goal scoring was essential to provide the team with the needed balance attack on offense, my coach's words led to doubt, which led to lesser play. From that point on, I rarely shot, and our opponents doubled their defense against our other scorers. As a result, we lost games that we could have won.

Even though I knew my scoring was vital to the team's success, I couldn't overcome the words of my coach. I didn't possess the mind muscle to do so.

As leaders, we must teach our team members the power of flexing their mind muscles daily so that they can overcome the messages from their past. Not only do we need to be able to think uniquely, problem solve, create, concentrate effectively, and expand ourselves, but we need our team members to do the same thing. We need to multiply ourselves through our teams so that we can double or quadruple our efforts.

Richard Serpa, VP, Mid-Market of Kyriba, and I spoke about the essentiality of coaching your team members. Richard earned his 6th degree black belt in Issinryu Karate, which is the degree where you are referred to as Hanshi or the teachers of teachers. He taught martial arts for 19 years. In 2006, Richard began training in Brazilian jiu-jitsu, a practice he continues to this day. Jiu-jitsu is like human chess, a cerebral art where you must think three moves ahead of your opponent. Because you are training versus a fully resistant opponent, you must be 100% focused and present. Richard described this practice as forced meditation.

In jiu-jitsu, you learn to be calm in the storm or become comfortable with the uncomfortable. In situational drills, you intentionally place yourself in a bad spot to figure out how to counter. From jiu-jitsu, Richard learned the power of thinking which he often shares with his team:

- Fighting is about timing.

- Good fighters find angles.

- Great fighters **create** the angles.

To create angles, you must practice perfect thinking. It is not enough to practice, because practice doesn't make perfect. *There are many people who waste time wrongly thinking, which places them in the wrong place at the wrong time with the wrong people. Perfect practice creates the opportunity to live in perfect timing with the right angles to win the goal.*

How do we teach right thinking?

First, our team members need to see the results of what right thinking does. We need to be the examples—the ones winning the chess game, thinking three moves ahead. We must be performing our mental push-ups daily.

What do mental push-ups look like? We know what a physical push-up looks like and many of us can't do those anymore, but we can always do mental push-ups.

In his jiu-jitsu practice, Richard must be fully present, focused in the here and now of a meditation practice so that any thoughts outside of the moment are abandoned. One of the best ways to exercise mental push-ups is to be more mindful of where our thoughts go and not allow the mind to decide what it wants to focus on. Meditation is a great practice to observe how much the mind wanders and how to bring the focus back on the breath.

We can bring this awareness with us all day. When a negative thought comes, we don't have to beat the thought out of us, let it come and release it.

The more effort put into stopping the thought, the more attention goes into the very thing unwanted.

A simple question to address the thought is: Is this thought serving me? If the answer is no, let it go.

When we teach our teams to observe and be curious about their thoughts, and that they have the power to release the thought, hold onto it, or increase its intensity, they own the power to increase their confidence and innovation.

Research by Dr. Sara Lazar from Harvard University indicated when we practice meditation daily our brains shrink in some areas and grow in other areas. Our brains expand in the ability to regulate emotions, concentrate, and remember. The brain declines in our flight and fight reactions, so through meditation push-ups we can have a sturdier, more elastic and agile mind.

Many athletic teams now include meditation as part of their daily practice schedules. So instead of ending a practice with free throws or conditioning, coaches provide 15 minutes for their athletes to meditate. Professional athletes like Lebron James, winner of four NBA MVP Awards, and Derek Jeter, a five-time

World Series champion, have utilized meditation, mindfulness, or yoga for improved concentration, better self-awareness, and stress reduction.

Schools have seen remarkable results in mindfulness practices such as Patterson High School who began a Mindful Movement Program in 2012. Rather than sending students to study hall, the administrators set up mindful movement time to reduce anger, frustration, and overwhelm. The practice resulted in 50% reduction in violent behavior, increased attendance, and higher GPAs.

Some of the top businesses in the country like Nike, Google, Sony, and Facebook have been leading the way in mindfulness training. Some businesses have included areas for stretching, relaxing, meditation, and yoga. Others have offered meditation classes, self-awareness, and self-mastery classes.

Giving our team members instruction on how to be mindful, meditate, or practice yoga or a martial art, and then allocating time for these mental push-ups is certain to benefit them. It might be a little bit outside of the norm, but then all greatness comes from bending or breaking the norm.

LEVERAGE THE WINNER'S FOCUS
The winner's focus refers to the power of thought.

We get what we put into our thought practices whether we want it or not.

We attract the things in our life through our attention and energy toward them. Whatever we focus on becomes the world we perceive and exist within.

Nothing exists without the thought of it first. Everything we see, hold, and experience appeared originally as a thought. Thoughts lead to action or to impasse. We either convince ourselves that we can or that we can't. This is the power of focus, because we choose the direction of our thoughts even if we are not aware of doing so.

What we place our focus on expands whether it is negative or positive. Our focus is like the law of gravity. Gravity doesn't change because we are a child without understanding the concept or later in life when we are eighty. If we fall as a two-year old from a counter, we are going to hit the ground. There is no magic between us and the kitchen floor. Gravity doesn't change when we understand it either. At eighty, if we lose balance on a ladder, we are going to hit the earth.

The reason people don't believe in the winner's focus is because they haven't examined it. They will "try" to focus on what they want by thinking about a huge check appearing in their mailbox. They concentrate on getting the check for a week and when the check doesn't show up, they believe thought focus is hoax.

Where their awareness fails is that the winner's focus doesn't work that way because they are not in alignment with the belief that the check will show up. They hope and wish the check will appear, but they don't believe that it will.

There is a gap between their belief and their desire. This is the true work behind the winner's focus—aligning our beliefs with our desires. We want something but don't think that we can have it.

If there is a distance between what we want and what we believe we can have, we cannot manifest our dreams.

We must focus on the winning operating systems that drive our actions. We have background thoughts that run without our attention to them. Those are the thoughts repeated thousands of times, which gives them incredible power over our actions. For example, we might not be aware of the thought beyond the desire. If we want a huge check to show up, but we focus most of our thoughts around poverty, not being able to pay our bills, and credit card debt, our belief system hovers around scarcity rather than wealth.

The key is to train ourselves to live in what we want rather than what is. If we can train our thoughts like Olympic Gold Medalists who see themselves winning the race hundreds of times before it is ever run, we have a much better chance of success.

If we want our team members to meet their goals, we must get their beliefs in alignment with their goals.

If their thoughts and feelings are in alignment with what they want to achieve, then nothing can stop them. This is where imagination is powerful. Train them to focus and visualize the result long before the result occurs. Play the game: What will you do when we **win** the sale, **finish** the project, **acquire** the next company, etc.?

> ## *The comparison that we should pay most attention to in our lives, the only one that really matters, is the relationship between our alignment between what we want and what we think we can have.*

Every time we meet as a staff, we could ask our team members to write down one thing they will do with the extra bonus money, the bonus vacation, etc. Have them share in one minute with a partner more details around the money, vacation, etc. Get them excited about the win versus the process.

Imagination is tied to belief and belief is needed to reach any goal.

In 2006, my basketball team was playing in the East Regional Tournament. We won the first round which put us into the Top 32 teams in the nation. Our next opponent, the Cardinals, was one of only two opponents who had beaten us all year, and we had defeated them narrowly seven days before in our conference tournament.

The Cardinals came to play with the goal of defeating us and getting to the Sweet Sixteen. They were playing in the zone, shooting a blistering 54% from the field and 72% from the three-point line. It felt like they couldn't miss a shot, and they rarely did.

We were struggling offensively and defensively but managed to keep the game close. Then our All-American, Lisa, a player who led us in points, blocked shots, rebounds, and defensive stops, fouled out of the game with four minutes to go.

That morning before the game we held a leadership meeting with our captains where we discussed the power of leading during times of adversity. We examined the benefits to the team when a player supported the team when she wasn't playing well. When Lisa fouled out, she became a coach on the sideline, yelling, cheering, and directing her teammates. Unknowingly, we had prepared for this very situation in our leadership huddle.

We fought to stay in the game with Lisa on the bench. Down by two points with less than 20 seconds left in the game, our point guard, Erica, drove to the basket for a lay-up. The ball spun around the rim and out. When the Cardinal post player grabbed the rebound, one of our players immediately fouled her.

The Cardinal player was on the foul line with two free throws and 13 seconds left in the game. If she made both free throws, our dream ended. As she was getting prepared to shoot the free throw, my players, standing next to the shooter on the foul line, looked at each other and said, "We've got this. This game is ours."

Imagine the audacity (i.e., confidence and alignment) of my team being two points down with 13 seconds to go, our best player on the bench, the Cardinals playing their best game of the year, their all-conference star at the free throw line, and us believing we could still win.

I stood on the sideline, staring at the scoreboard, the time, and the score, knowing in my heart that we were going to win. I didn't know how, but I knew, like my players did, that this game was ours.

The Cardinal player missed the first free throw. When she missed the second free throw, we grabbed the rebound. Erica, who had just missed the tie-scoring lay-up possessed the basketball. She dribbled the ball off the back foot of a teammate, almost lost the ball, then recovered it. Then, she fell on her knees, but managed to continue dribbling the ball. When she got up, with time dwindling down, she sprinted to the basket. With three seconds remaining, and their 6'3" post player in perfect position to block Erica's shot, she dished it to a teammate who made the basket, tying the score as the buzzer sounded.

The game went into a five-minute overtime where the lead changed three times. Despite our All-American being on the bench, we played with confidence and in alignment with our goal. With eight seconds remaining in overtime, Courtney drove to the basket and made a jump shot placing us in the lead for good.

Our responsibility as leaders is to hold the vision, the dream, and the goal in our minds and keep it real in the minds of our team members.

The reason we won this game is because we knew that we were going to win. It didn't matter that the other team played the best game of their lives. It didn't matter that our All-American was on the bench. It didn't matter that our point guard fell to the floor twice with 13 seconds to go.

We all believed that we were going to win. This is the power of aligning beliefs with desires.

By teaching the winner's focus and how to align our feelings and thoughts with our desires, we empower our teams to live their dreams.

STOP THE CHAOS

Life is messy, unpredictable, erratic, and fickle. When we stand in what feels like chaos and succumb to the feelings associated with chaos, then we can't find our way forward. We are stuck in the vacillating events around us. This is when stress becomes almost unbearable.

Our team members will face chaos. This is not an **if** but a **when**. The chaos might be at work, or it might be the result of an event at home. Either way, if they fail to understand that there is an option to embrace chaos, then they will become anxious, impatient, gloomy, despondent, distressed, or melancholy.

One of my coaching clients, "April," lost a half-acre of land which included a shed, huge trees, and half of a workshop during an unprecedented flood. The loss along with the hassle of dealing with insurance, FEMA, and other environmental protection agencies caused her to suffer from anxiety.

April said, "If I can hold onto anxiety, then I won't feel depressed. I'm clinging to anxiety because the other option will completely defeat me."

I said, "How does it feel to believe that anxiety and depression are your only two options?"

April emitted a small, forced laugh. "Shitty."

"Understandable. Because shitty doesn't feel good. What are some other emotional options?"

"Anger, rage, fury."

I said, "Well, believe it or not, anger is better than depression."

April said, "How so?"

"When you feel depressed, what actions are you most likely to take?"

April emitted a forced laugh again. "Over-medicating with beer, eating Cheetos, watching sappy, sad movies which would make me have another beer and a second bag of Cheetos."

"How does that make you feel?"

April said, "Shitty. That seems to be my patent answer here."

"That is okay. Admitting an emotion is a good thing because you know where you are. Now, what would change if you felt angry?"

"You really don't want me to go there. Anger would cause me to yell at the insurance folks, sledgehammer the half of my house that is remaining, and exercise until I passed out."

I responded, "How does anger feel different than anxiety?"

"Besides the need to sledgehammer walls and some people?"

I laughed. "Yes."

"The main difference is that I would be doing something rather than feeling hopeless."

I said, "How does it feel to release hopelessness?"

April said, "Well, I really like beer and Cheetos."

I chuckled again. "You don't have to give up beer and Cheetos...and they don't have to be associated with anxiety, depression, and sad, sappy emotions."

April responded, "Well if I can keep my Cheetos and beer, then doing something toward a better outcome would feel better."

"That is the first step. Getting out of the need to numb yourself."

April's face clouded with suspicion. "What is the second step? You are not going to take away my beer, are you?"

"No. What if you just embraced each moment as it came? You don't have to sledgehammer anything, including the insurance agents. Just be in the moment. Accept what is without judgment."

April retorted, "You want me to do what? Accept without judgment? That, my friend, is impossible. I lost furniture, shoes, tools, refrigerators, my brand-new oven, our hot tub. Should I go on?"

"How does that make you feel when you think about all that you lost."

"We are back to shitty again. Where are those Cheetos?"

I answered, "I understand that you like to use laughter to undermine anxiety, which is okay. What if you could let go of all your stuff and the struggle so that you could rest for a few minutes? What would that do for you?"

"It would feel amazing to let go of what was lost and to stop fretting about the future."

"Yes...and that is the choice."

April said, "But the flood really happened. Am I just supposed to believe that it didn't?"

"No. Of course not. But the emotions that have you in their grasp don't feel good and they are causing suffering. If you choose to rest in what is, would those feelings go away allowing you to move with less stress? What would that do for you?"

April retorted, "Here we go again with you wanting me to let go of beer and Cheetos." She laughed and then said, "I understand. I am where I am. If I accept that, there is less suffering and with less suffering, I can think and move more efficiently."

"Yes. How have your emotions affected your job as the leader of your team?"

"Oh boy! I am certain that my team feels as if I have been a sledgehammer on their emotions the past two weeks, which is unfair to them. I don't want to do that any longer."

"The key here is to understand that you are working against yourself, which never feels good.

You cannot undo what has been done. What you can do is focus on letting go of all that you cannot change."

"Ah...yes. Yoda speaks again. Be in the now. Let go. Surrender... and drink a couple of beers."

"It is more than being in the now. It is trusting that you are in the process of becoming more and experiencing more. It is knowing that what is happening now is a needed component of the wiser and more compassionate you."

April sighed. "Surrender and trust. In theory, those components sound easy when we talk about them, but in practice, they are not so easy."

"So, it is easier to be depressed and angry than surrendering the thoughts that create those emotions?"

191

"Yeah. I've always gravitated to negative emotions when things go a little sideways. I don't have the toolset to be calm among the storms."

I said, "Up until now."

April replied, "Yes, up until now."

When April practiced letting go and being okay with what was in the moment, she found more peace and with that peace, was able to have more productive conversations with her partner and her team members at work. Her calmness through adverse times became a hallmark of her leadership causing her superiors to notice her abilities. They began coming to her for mentorship which led to her becoming their leader.

> ***Embracing chaos is the ability to know that the challenge and solution exist simultaneously, because the move forward cannot exist without the challenge that propels us to do so.***

When we can rest in assurance as events crumble around us, then our thoughts are sharper leading to healthier actions.

We can teach our team members the wisdom we've acquired over time. We don't have to shove beliefs on them; we can share what has given us the capacity to be happy within our circumstances. Our folks can choose what works for them and what doesn't work for them, but if they are unaware of the tools we use, then they have no option but to live in chaos.

Embracing chaos is the not the same as giving up. Giving up means we are not moving forward and unwilling to act in a beneficial manner. Embracing the situation allows us to stop the negative emotions so that we gain clarity around how we can profit from the situation.

To receive the unexpected gains from a challenging situation, we must accept the unanticipated losses even though we didn't want them, don't like them, and would have preferred a better outcome. This is where gratitude has its biggest impact—to be grateful that things are not worse. We can choose the better feeling and live there rather than eating five bags of Cheetos, drinking a case of beer, and binge watching sad, sappy movies.

BE AN APPRECIATION MAGNET

During an interview with Breana Chan, VP of Global Supplier Diversity at JP Morgan, Breana discussed the power of being an appreciation magnet. At first glance, Breana had everything to be appreciative for: a speaker who has shared the stage with Mark Wahlberg, John Travolta, and Mel Gibson, an author of the book, *Build a Business Not A Hobby: Six Easy Steps to Success*, and a successful businesswoman who was named by Ernst and Young as #11 in the top 100 women in procurement.

When we see ultra-successful people, our perception is that they should be soaking in thankfulness, because they have it easy. But life is not made of easy pathways, and when we get a deeper picture of the lives of other people, we are often surprised at their challenges and how they've navigated them.

Breana's second child, Helen, got sick with a mal-rotated intestine, an extremely rare health complication. Helen suffered one medical emergency after another. The doctors finally found an answer, a gastric pacemaker which allows her to eat and process food. The disease is so rare that Helen was only the 61st patient to receive one.

The gastric pacemaker technology is thirty years behind most medical technology which means that there is no way to monitor if the pacemaker is working. The only means to determine if the pacemaker is failing is Helen's health. If she doesn't feel well and can't process food, she must head back to the surgeon immediately.

When Helen first became sick, Breana was hot tempered, easily triggered, and took things personally. It was Helen's illness that turned Breana toward appreciation of the good things in life. When Helen was in the hospital, Breana made the conscious decision to post only thankful messages on Facebook. When the nurses woke them up countless times in the middle of the night to check vitals, instead of being angry at their interruption which disrupted much-need rest, she was thankful for their diligence. When medical bills rolled in, she was grateful that she could pay for them.

Breana quit griping about challenges that life threw at her, replacing angst and anger with appreciation. She turned to The

Higher Power with thankfulness, which gave her greater joy and happiness. The more that she spoon-fed herself gratitude, the more those around her found goodness in their lives.

Practicing appreciation daily produces positive effects on us and our team members. Gratitude is a fountain of optimism which enhances our emotional and physical well-being. It propels cooperation and collaboration, providing the necessary foundation for enhanced teamwork.

Appreciation is a learned behavior, an approach to leadership and life that requires intentionality. Because gratitude has the power to positively affect our attitudes which in turn influences our well-being, it makes sense to develop an attitude of appreciation.

When we understand that we have choices at how we look at things, and when we choose to be grateful for what has occurred rather than angry, we search for better thoughts which lead to better actions. Appreciation leads to happiness and happy people are more productive.

To revolutionize our leadership, live in and teach appreciation, because the response to gratitude is invariably positive.

When we show thankfulness to those around us, the appreciation is reciprocated through respect. Because appreciation is seen as a feature of integrity and goodness, our teams admire those who embody it.

Appreciation is an important part of leadership because it helps people feel connected to their work and motivated to do their best. When leaders show gratitude towards their team members, it sends a strong message about how important they consider them and how committed they are to creating a positive environment for everyone working together.

Research has indicated that appreciation can enhance physical health, multiply resiliency, improve sleep, augment energy, boost life satisfaction, and expand patience, humility, and wisdom. If those reasons are not enough to practice more gratitude, it also encourages positive relationships, strengthens constructive social behaviors, and promotes job satisfaction.

When presenting breakout sessions for companies, I often ask the attendees, "How do you teach appreciation?" Most of the attendees' answer, "By example." Yes, this is true, but leading by example is never enough. *You must teach people what you want them to know, because some people can't extrapolate through an example to the knowledge that you want them to possess.*

To create an optimal effect from appreciation, follow these seven strategies:

1. **Build a winning scoreboard.** This could be a virtual scoreboard where each team member starts the day by recording a win from the previous day. You can denote categories for wins such as wins from teammates, the department, the company, or a personal victory.

2. **Write a victory text to a team member.** Each week write a short text or an email to a team member thanking them for a victory they contributed to the team.

3. **Gold medal your team wins.** Establish a tradition of celebrating your wins, which can be as simple as virtual or live high-fives. One sales company that I worked with created a gold medal ceremony at the end of each week. The highest sales team received chocolate gold medals. At the end of the month, the team with the most gold medals received a bonus.

4. **End each staff meeting with a winning circle.** We want people to feel good at the end of every meeting, so that they bring those feelings forward to the day. The more your team members associate fun with meetings, the more likely they will look forward to the next one. Before the meeting is over, ask each person to quickly state one event, person, or win that occurred between the last meeting and this one.

5. **Celebrate your challenges.** Once a month, ask each team member to state one challenge that they've had. Then, have them acknowledge how the challenge has moved them forward.

6. **Ask your team to do a daily mental push-up log.** Ask them to write down five new things that they are thankful for each day. Once a month, ask them to share one day of their logs with the team.

7. **Create Mystery Motivators for 7 days during challenging times**. Each day the mystery motivator will give a small present to the person they drew as a partner. The "present" could be a shared quote, a page from a book, a YouTube video, etc. At the end of the seven days, ask each team member to share one appreciation they had for the experience from either giving or receiving.

Breana said, "You must find and keep the mindset that the hurdle in front of you is the thing that keeps you from success, so you can't stop at the hurdle." Look at the hurdle with thankfulness and the hurdle changes forms. Most people stop at the hurdle and get mad at the circumstances and people that appear to be the problem, but once thankfulness is the go-to answer, the naysaying disappears replaced with energy to conquer.

LIVE IN THE SUCCESS ZONE

You've probably met people who seem like they get everything they want, and you have two choices when you meet those folks. The first one is to be jealous, wanting what they have, thinking that you deserve more than them, and being mad at them for having what you want. This type of thinking doesn't deter their success and hinders yours.

The second way to view their success is to align with it. This is the success zone—aligning your will with their success. You watch them, take notes, ask questions, and imagine yourself living the life that they have.

Many of our team members choose to live in jealousy rather than aligning with the success zone. Jealousy is what drives silos, indifference, and anger.

The success zone is where people climb up the ladder of positive vibrations, which means they spend less time in low self-esteem, self-recrimination, hopelessness, regret, fear, anger, insatiable needs, resentment, and outside motivators. The people who thrive in the success zone breathe empowerment, flexibility, acceptance, self-validation, self-correction, emotional calmness, and unconditional love for themselves and others. In the success zone, there is nothing to prove and no comparisons.

This is the space where people understand their true powers as creators and experiences of their lives. They live in harmony with nature and other people. They understand that nobody else has the power to make them feel any emotion, so their happiness is 100% dependent upon their views of the world.

Imagine a world full of people who are genuinely friendly, open-minded, committed to supporting others, willing to face their inner issues, and see all people as coming from the same source so there is no reason for judgment or comparison. This would be a utopia of human kindness, and while utopias are figments of our imaginations; our imaginations are the way toward utopias.

We are limited by our humanness, but within our human capacity is the ability to share our paths to wisdom. With every conversation, we can open a new door of thought. With every staff meeting, we can insert a fresh insight on conflicts. With every leadership retreat, we can share best practices. With our discretionary funds, we can offer our teams access to books, educational sessions, and coaches.

We may not create a utopia, but we can funnel awareness to our team members that will shape a better team and organization.

BE CURIOUS

Matt Bronniman is the SVP of Business Development at Overture and a man who took time stepping into the leadership role, but once he got there, he understood the power of being curious. Through the interviewing process for this book, Matt and I chatted about his journey into leadership.

At the age of 16, he enrolled into the British Army where he remained as a basic soldier. When presented with an opportunity to be a commissioned officer, he told the army officers that he wasn't interested. He preferred to hang out with the "crap pot" squad, a group of his buddies who enjoyed whining and complaining about their leaders.

At the age of 28, still employed as a basic army solider, Matt decided to leave the army. On the day of his departure, he was again asked to become an officer. Without hesitation, Matt declined. He didn't see himself as a leader.

Matt became a frozen food salesman knocking on doors to sell his goods. One day, his father having seen his son in a role less than his full potential, grabbed Matt and exclaimed, "Son, you are not doing anything!"

Matt responded, "Yes, I am. I am making good money."

His father said, "No, you are not. You are barely scraping by."

Recognizing the truth in his father's words, Matt joined a telecommunications company where he began installing equipment. Within a couple of years, Matt was asked to take on a team leadership role with 33 people on his team. Matt told me, "Fortunately, I didn't have any formal textbook leadership training, so I learned to be curious. When I didn't know something, which was often, I asked my team how to do it."

Matt utilized the power of curiosity combined with listening to empower his team to act on their expertise. Matt understood that his job was to set deadlines and expectations, empower his team through questions, and hold them accountable for getting the job done correctly and on time.

After a couple of years as a team lead, Matt and a friend decided to create their own company. He didn't know how to get contracts so he cold-called Alcatel, a mobile phone and devices company. A company leader explained to Matt that they couldn't give him any contracts, because it took two years of training on the equipment before they could hire anybody.

Instead of admitting defeat, Matt became curious wondering what it would take to get the contract. So, he talked to his old team of 33 engineers and asked them to join his company. Thirty team members said yes.

Then Matt wondered, "How am I going to feed these people?"

He called Alcatel back and told them he wanted to fulfill a contract. They responded that they had already explained to him the training needed.

Matt said, "Well, you are not going to be able to do anything without me."

The people from Alcatel asked, "How is that?"

Matt said, "I've got all your engineers."

Curious leaders like Matt ask never-ending questions of ourselves and our team members. We want to hear our team members' opinions, why they feel strongly about them, what their suggestions are, and what will occur due to their suggestions. Curiosity guides us to more meaningful dialogue with our teams, which leads to trust and inspiration.

One of the skills of curiosity is looking at old things with a new mind, which means not accepting the status quo of ordinary policies, procedures, or equipment.

Often we don't see what is in front of us because we've accepted it without inquiry.

Curious leaders revisit standard practices often asking questions like:

- How does this practice (procedure, policy, software, equipment) hinder us from moving forward?

- Is there a better way to do what we've always done?

- Is there a good reason to keep doing what we've been doing?

- Can we make this more effective and efficient?

- If you were to make changes in our policies, what would they be?

- Open the dialogue with the question, "What if?" What if we could build a software program that enabled us to do X, Y, or Z?" What if we could scale our business to a billion dollars?"

- What would it take to complete our what if dreams?

Teaching curiosity permits people to be curious and encourages people to do so. When we stop having a "yeah but" mentality of why something won't work and instead create a "yeah and" mentality of let's explore how it will work, your team will naturally become more innovative.

To further grow curiosity, teach your team to:

- Ask exploratory, non-aggressive questions. Instead of asking, "Why did you approach our client that way?" Ask, "Please walk me through your thought process of speaking with our client."

- Pause after asking questions to allow for further explanations.

- Ask follow-up questions.

- Ask for their suggestions of how to do it *even* better.

- Remember that what you don't know about somebody could be the reason why they are underperforming. Be curious about who they are and why they do what they do.

- Before offering advice, ask if they want it. "Would it be okay if I shared with you something that I've learned?"

- Abandon judgment for curiosity. Instead of believing people aren't smart enough or talented enough, ask them questions. Discover what their genius is.

Trash the old idea that curiosity killed the cat, because we are not cats and the saying kills innovation. Curiosity is what fuels the mind; it is what drives us to new awareness. The more we focus on building curiosity within our teams, the more we will be the company that other leaders aspire to have.

GIVING OUR KNOWLEDGE AWAY IS OUR BIGGEST GIFT BACK TO OURSELVES

Understanding how influential we are is essential to the power that we can give away. While we cannot make our team members wiser, smarter, or more powerful, we can introduce them to concepts that will give them the opportunity to thrive.

If we keep our knowledge like my Coach Bud did, then we produce weaker teams. Our power is fully recognized when our team members exceed our abilities. During the last two years I was a college basketball coach, one of my players, Lindsey, was on the brink of breaking some of my college records which had stood for more than 20 years.

The president of the university asked me, "Are you going to be upset when Lindsey breaks your records?"

I answered, "Why would I be? It would be the greatest honor I could imagine."

This is our greatest accomplishment as leaders—to grow to the extent that no matter what we give away to others, we have more within ourselves to give.

WINNING SUCCESS STEPS

1. What are two practices that will enable your team to flex their mind muscles?
2. List two ways you can bridge the gap between what your team members want and what they believe they can have.
3. What three methods can you utilize to embrace the chaos so that challenging times don't stop your team's productivity?
4. What are two gratitude traditions you will establish to keep a positive culture?
5. What are three best disciplines for building and maintaining a team of curiosity?

WINNING TAKEAWAYS

- Productivity is always the result of what we think, and if we think we are at full capacity, then we are stuck living the life we've created in our minds.
- If we cannot adapt, we will not succeed.
- Those trivial things that we see as essential take up residency in our minds which become too full of trivia to allow for better opportunities.
- There are many people who waste time wrongly thinking, which places them in the wrong place at the wrong time with the wrong people.
- The more effort put into stopping the thought, the more attention goes into the very thing unwanted.
- The comparison that we should pay most attention to in our lives, the only one that really matters, is the relationship between our alignment between what we want and what we think we can have.
- You cannot undo what has been done. What you can do is focus on letting go of all that you cannot change.
- Embracing chaos is the ability to know that the challenge and solution exist simultaneously, because the move forward cannot exist without the challenge that propels us to do so.
- Teach people what you want them to know, because some people can't extrapolate through an example to the knowledge that you want them to possess.
- Often we don't see what is in front of us because we've accepted it without inquiry.

WINNING QUOTES

"Never satisfy your fear during times of trials and tribulations. Look for and live in the opportunities that arise from them."
Mike King, CEO of Volunteers of America

"It is easy to blame circumstances on other people, but you have the right to work harder to get anything you want."
Bert Kuntz, Owner, Bison Union Coffee

"Understand what has shaped and formed you and whether that is a good thing or not. If it a negative, change who you are and how you lead."
Marie Olson, Executive Operation Director, Sound Transit

"Broadcast your core values, hold people accountable to those values, and allow your leadership teams to hold people accountable. Hire, fire, and reward people based on your core values."
Ryan Gregory, CEO, Wyoming Roofing

"You must create a reason so big that obstacles don't matter."
Eric Tarr, CEO of Generations Physical Therapy

"Leaders who have been successful develop the right strategy. They tap into the institutional knowledge before realigning people, refocusing efforts, or altering processes. They focus on building a culture where people are valued, respected, and trusted before making changes."
Marty Roth, President, University of Charleston

"The best way to deal with challenging team members is to ask them questions that reveal their questions to themselves."
Jamie Cozby, CEO, Keller Williams Yellowstone Properties

"We must have a bigger picture than ourselves and get over thinking me-me-me to shift thoughts to we-we-we."
Marv Hodges, Division Leader, PFS Investments

"Leaders must be willing to find solutions in places where other people thought it was impossible."
Michelle Boxx, CEO, Boxxbury

"You must inspect what you expect."
Richard Lowe, President/CEO of Franchise Services

"You must engage in unfiltered conflict with your team to hold yourself and your team accountable. You might have less interactions but far deeper ones."
Luis Lemaitre, Group VP, Oracle, North American Cloud

"You've got to be okay with things not going the way you've planned just as long as you've gained knowledge from it."
Damon Groethe, VP, Knowledge Services

"The most dangerous words in business are that we've always done it this way. You must get people out of thinking that way."
Marc Ashworth, CIO, First Bank, Greater St. Louis

"One of the biggest challenges leaders face is to defuse flawed emotions."
Kartik Shankar, SVP Engineering, Jefferies

"You must acknowledge that disagreement is okay and understand that more disagreement leads to more engagement."
Samuel Seisdedos, VP and Head of Operations, Ericsson

"Explain the why behind each action to your team members so that they will get on board with the projects and processes."
Tim Patneadue, EVP, COO, HSA Bank

"The way to create a great company is to talk to all your people, especially the front-line workers. They will tell you what is frustrating and what is working."
Norman Frederick, VP, SVP, Partner, NTT Data Services

"We must strive to see the best in all folks. Believe in them. Give them the benefit of the doubt. Coach them up and if they are not the right fit, let them go."
Art Smuck, President/CEO, FedEx Supply Chain (retired)

"One of the best things you can do to move your company forward is to hire the right people and fire the wrong ones."
Chuck Warshaver, CEO Coach, Board Member

"Become a student of feedback. The response from your team and management is your report card."
Steve Goodenow, President/CEO, Goodenow Bancorporation

"You are the culture coach of your company. You are there to provide guidance, to support people through challenges, and to help them find the root issue of their challenges."
Lisa King, CEO, Magnifi U

"My job as a leader is to take the arrows and bullets for my team and to remove their obstacles so that they can be successful."
David George, CEO, Pixability

"Hero-based organizations can only scale if they scale the hero."
Rich Sheridan, CEO, Menlo Innovations

Making The Hard Easier

Leadership is challenging. Every day there is another software glitch, the departure of a prominent team member, an upset client, the restructuring of a department, a U-turn in strategies, the termination of a team member, or a major miscommunication. The reason that we are in leadership is for moments like these because other people can't handle the everyday emergencies that occur.

We are in our positions to make the hard easier because other people cannot. We understand that with every championship team there are mountains to summit, oceans to navigate, and the unknown to discover. We must be resilient, because no matter what is in front of us, our capacity to forge ahead is the impetus for our teams to follow us.

Whether we like it or not, our teams mimic our behaviors.

We must find the personal and professional maturity that allows us to bend without breaking and to stand firm when the winds are howling around us. We are more than adult babysitters; we are the coaches of positive change.

We must learn to master our emotions, thoughts, and behaviors so that we can teach others the benefits of overseeing themselves. Imagine the power of influencing people to discard their victim mentalities, so that they can take responsibility for their own behaviors and outcomes. Imagine showing team members how to overcome their need to self-sabotage. Imagine teaching team members how to opt for conversation rather than anger or frustration.

While we are not gods or goddesses, we can shift the thinking of our team members one inch at a time so that the inches turn into miles. While we are not generals in a war, we are generals in the everyday human struggles which propel our communities toward better decisions. Our battleground is not written about, covered in the *New York Times*, or discussed on national television, but it is essential to the American dream.

THE TRUE VALUE OF WINNING LEADERSHIP

Once we have evolved with the awareness that leadership is not about power; it is about empowering others, we rate our leadership on how we've impacted others. What we discover along our journey from the designation of leader to legacy-maker is that money, titles, and power don't mean that much.

We make the hard easier by building cultures where people know that it is their right to question, challenge, and to say no. We think beyond the evident, beyond the facts and look for the things that nobody else is looking for. When we live in this zone of winning leadership, we are the innovators, the creators, and the thought leaders.

Our success is based on how our people evolve and who they become. We marvel at their new roles, their climbs up the corporate ladder, and how the ones who we once taught are now teaching us.

Throughout this book, you have been exposed to winning leadership skillsets. To produce winning organizations, it is no longer enough to survey people about what they want and then provide it, because this way of thinking produces short-term results. While it is good to understand what people want and to examine if their needs line up with what is best for the company, sometimes giving them what they think they want is conveying the message that impressive results come from altering reality, not self-development.

Winning leadership is about confronting and interrupting nonproductive thinking. Winning leaders *create self-awareness*, ask questions that cause deep reflection, support people in finding new truths, and call people to excellence. We *don't allow them to live in toxic thinking;* we force them to examine their hurt feelings, gossip, defensiveness, complaining, judging, and comparing.

When we demand that our team members become better people, not just better employees, we are truly winning the game of life. We learn what is valuable.

We hold golden the notes, the visits, and the emails of appreciation that we receive. When one of our team members thanks us for teaching them how to focus on the winning factors, to see success as an adventure, to build collaboration, to slash excuses, or how to be a champion of life, we feel the ultimate rewards of leadership.

We might throw away our plaques, certificates, and awards as the years pass, but most of us keep the notes, letters, and emails of appreciation.

We understand the true evidence of winning leadership is in the words and actions of gratitude received from our team members.

My dream is that one day we will understand that our role as leaders is to create winning team members who are resilient, adaptable, growth-oriented, reflective, positive, and capable of sharing their learned behaviors with others.

WINNING SUCCESS STEPS

1. What are two behaviors you are going to adopt because of reading this book?
2. What are five characteristics that make you a winning leader?
3. What do you need to change in your culture so that you are creating a legacy which will alter the way leadership is viewed?

WINNING TAKEAWAYS

- One of the best ways to increase the insights of our team members is to not allow them to take the easiest road, but to forge ahead through the biggest obstacles

and to empower them to believe they have the skills
to do so.

- Our team members are watching us, and they are
more likely to mimic what we live than what we say.
- Winning leaders create self-awareness, ask questions
that cause deep reflection, support people in finding
new truths, and call people to excellence.

Acknowledgments For
the Wisdom in This Book

I would like to express my special thanks of gratitude to leaders who shared their insights, wisdom, quotes, and thoughts with me. I was impressed with the number of leaders who believed in growing their team members through webinars, seminars, coaching, and one-on-one meetings. My hope for positive and impactful leaders has grown throughout the interviews by listening to the desire for personal and professional growth. I am blessed by the leaders who participated in this book, and I hope that their wisdom supports your growth.

Alan Rogers, Chair, Board of Advisors, Center for Leadership, UC-Boulder

https://www.linkedin.com/in/alan-rogers-a5575/

Alesha Webb, President, Village Bank,

https://www.linkedin.com/company/villagebank/

Amanda Wiles

https://www.linkedin.com/in/amandawiles/

Andrew Laudato, COO, The Vitamin Shoppe

https://www.linkedin.com/in/andrewlaudato/

Andrew Newman, Owner at Newman Restoration & Cleaning

https://www.linkedin.com/in/andrew-newman-28230384/

Anne Warner Cribbs, President/CEO, Bay Area Sports Organizing Committee

https://www.linkedin.com/in/anne-warner-cribbs-6b656312/.

Art Smuck, CEO/President, FedEx Supply Chain (retired)

https://www.linkedin.com/in/artsmuck/

Ashley Wiseman, Executive Director of Greenhouse Solutions Foundation

https://www.linkedin.com/in/awsustainabilitycatalyst/

Ashwin Bharath, CEO of Revature

https://www.linkedin.com/in/ashwin-bharath-a475a17/

Atiya Hamilton, CEO, Blue/Green Marketing

https://www.linkedin.com/in/atiya-hamilton-52174b51/

Barbara Morrison, Founder, and President of TMC Financing

https://www.linkedin.com/in/barbaramorrisontmc/

Benita Fitzgerald, Olympian, Vice-President, League Apps

https://www.linkedin.com/in/benitafitzgeraldmosleyol/

Bert Kuntz, Owner, Bison Union Coffee,

https://www.linkedin.com/in/bert-kuntz-16094422/

Beth Ford, President and CEO at Land O'Lakes, Inc.

https://www.linkedin.com/in/bethfordlol/

Bill Klevenberg, CEO of Helpdesk

https://www.linkedin.com/in/elitenetworks/

Blake Howitt, RVP Experience Management at SAP

https://www.linkedin.com/in/blakehowitt/

Bob Miller, President/CEO, One10

https://www.linkedin.com/in/bob-miller-115b6410/

Bob Steensma, CEO of Five Star
https://www.linkedin.com/in/bob-steensma-baa60b47/
Bob Yates, Former SVP of Level 3Communications, City Council Member
Brian Lipscomb, CEO at Energy Keepers Inc.
https://www.linkedin.com/in/brian-lipscomb-05546b5a/
Brain Waldron, President, and CEO, Dort Financial Credit Union
https://www.linkedin.com/in/brian-waldron-61ba5653/
Breana Chan, VP, Global Supplier Diversity at JP Morgan Chase & Co.
https://www.linkedin.com/in/breanachan/
Brenda Weatherby, Director of People & Culture, Weatherby, Inc.
https://www.linkedin.com/in/brenda-weatherby-a9448247/
Carla Borsoi, Head of Business Operations, Felt
https://www.linkedin.com/in/carlaborsoi/
Carrie O'Brien, CIO of J&J, (retired)
https://www.linkedin.com/in/carrieobrien4/
Carol Houle, SVP, Global Head of Financial Services and Insurance at Atos
https://www.linkedin.com/in/carolhoule/
Carol Spector Riegert, SVP/CIO, Oxford Global Resources
https://www.linkedin.com/in/carolspectorriegert/
C. David Kikumoto, Founder and Chairman of the Board, Denver Management Advisors, Inc.
https://www.linkedin.com/in/c-david-kikumoto-66270020/
Chad Greenleaf, SVP, Client Services at AppsFlyer
https://www.linkedin.com/in/chadgreenleaf/
Charles Dickens IV, Equity Compliance, Corporate Wellness, Consultant
https://www.linkedin.com/in/charles-dickens-iv-311197103/
Cheryl Silverman, VP of IT, First American Property and Casualty (retired)
https://www.linkedin.com/in/cherylsilverman/

Christy Elliott, VP of BB&T, Charleston, WV
https://www.linkedin.com/in/christy-elliott-bly-b2153a9/
Chuck Tooley, President, Tooley Communications
https://www.linkedin.com/in/chuck-tooley-6346747/
Claire Darley, VP, Digital Media Field Sales & WW Customer Support, Adobe
https://www.linkedin.com/in/clairedarley/
Coralee Schmitz, COO of Rimrock
https://www.linkedin.com/in/coralee-schmitz-3216695b/
Cori Cook, CEO, Veza Heath
Craig McLaughlin, CEO, Extractable
https://www.linkedin.com/in/mclaughlincraig/
Crystal Stanfield, VP Global Talent Acquisition, Cboe
https://www.linkedin.com/in/crystalstanfield/
Cynthia Persily, Vice Chancellor for Health Sciences at WV
https://www.linkedin.com/in/cynthia-persily-5b3b5823/
Damon Groethe, VP, Knowledge Services
https://www.linkedin.com/in/damongrothe/
Danny Wyrwas, Owner, Absolute Fence, Elevate Leadership & Business Consulting
https://www.linkedin.com/in/danny-wyrwas-26868a22/
Darius McDougle, VP of Digital Marketing, Antenna
https://www.linkedin.com/in/dariusmcdougle/
Dave Nguyen, Founder and Chief of Solutions, TRU IP, LLC
https://www.linkedin.com/in/davenguyen/
David Bell, CEO, Alps Insurance
https://www.linkedin.com/in/david-bell-0542ab8/
David Flint, Co-Creator and Chief Executive Educator, Value Creation Co.
https://www.linkedin.com/in/david-flint-594b00/
David George, CEO, Pixability
https://www.linkedin.com/company/pixability/?original Subdomain=ws
David J. Jacowitz, President, Evolution Financial Group
https://www.linkedin.com/in/davidjacowitz/

Dean Bushey, SVP Sustainability, TravelCenters of America
https://www.linkedin.com/in/dean-bushey/
Donna DeVarona, Olympian, President at DAMAR Productions
https://www.linkedin.com/in/donna-devarona-ba667517/
Dr. Charcora Palmer, CEO, Total Power Financial Solutions LLC
https://www.linkedin.com/in/charcorapalmer/   Dr. Paul Gavoni, COO BDI Media
https://www.linkedin.com/in/paul-paulie-gavoni-ed-d-bcba-60600843/details/experience/
Elaine McNeil, VP of Loreal (deceased)
Eric Schreimann, CEO, Club Fitness
https://www.linkedin.com/in/eric-schreimann-9b919aa4/
Eric Tarr, CEO of Generations Physical Therapy
https://www.linkedin.com/in/eric-tarr-pt-dpt-mba-ocs-49b06b36/
George Soule, Partner at Soule & Stull LLC,
https://www.linkedin.com/in/george-soule-3926085/
Ginny Chappell, Fintech Leader, Digital Payments and Banking, Board Member
https://www.linkedin.com/in/ginny-chappell-94047110/
Gordon Pry, CFO of Sportsman's Alliance, Executive Officer, US Army Reserves https://www.linkedin.com/in/gordon-pry-9a51924/
Gordon Riggle, Chancellor's Advisory Board for the Center of Leadership at UC-Boulder
https://www.linkedin.com/in/gordon-riggle-2b85606/
Gregory Green, Co-Founder, Director, Equity Holder, Fatbeam
https://www.linkedin.com/in/gregory-green-1a40793/
Greg Katcher, Owner at CHAT of Michigan, Inc.
https://www.linkedin.com/in/chatofmichigan/
Greg McCall, Owner, McCall Homes, McCall Development
https://www.linkedin.com/in/greg-mccall-b459841
Gregory VanDyke, Executive Level Leader, Stratify Technologies
https://www.linkedin.com/in/gregoryvandyke1643/
Harold Hughes, SVP of PNC
https://www.linkedin.com/in/harold-hughes/

Hayden Thomas, Founder & CEO, Paird
https://www.linkedin.com/in/hayden-thomas-bba6762/
Jack Elder, CEO of Oregon Olympics
https://www.linkedin.com/in/jack-elder-2b435937/
James Binder, CEO, Co-Founder, Stiddle
https://www.linkedin.com/company/stiddle/
James McCormick, Military and Veterans Affairs Director
https://www.linkedin.com/in/james-mccormick-d-d-csp-drone-pilot-bb134913/
Jamie Cozby, CEO, Keller Williams Yellowstone Properties
https://www.linkedin.com/in/jamie-cozby-00b4981b/
Jason Knickerbocker, Owner Tax Scout, Co-Founder of BeWizeApp   https://www.linkedin.com/in/jason-knickerbocker-68096619a/
Jason Hawkins, CEO of First United Bank
https://www.linkedin.com/in/jjasonhawkins/
Jay Mattern, CEO, Villing+Company and TerraFirma Marketing
https://www.linkedin.com/in/jaymattern/
Jay Tkachuk, SVP Digital Services
https://www.linkedin.com/in/jaytkachuk/
Jayme Hill, COO, Diamond Media Solutions Inc.
https://www.linkedin.com/in/jayme-hill-gardner/
Jeff Carroll, Former H.S. Volleyball Coach, Townsend Leadership Coach   https://www.linkedin.com/in/jeff-carroll-93849072/

Jeff Heggie, Success Coach, Mortgage Specialist
https://www.linkedin.com/in/jeffheggie/
Jeff Newgard, CEO, Bank of Idaho
https://www.linkedin.com/in/jeffnewgard/
Jeff Walters, CEO, Community Financial Group
https://www.linkedin.com/in/jeff-walters-34668188/

Jeffrey Bissoy, Founder of the Plugged App
https://www.linkedin.com/in/jeffbis/
Jennifer Bagley, CEO, CI Web Group, Inc.0
https://www.linkedin.com/in/jenniferbagley/
Jennifer Bertetto, CEO at Trib Total Media and 535media
https://www.linkedin.com/in/jenniferbertetto/

Jennifer L Lovett, President/CEO Crystal Financial Insurance Services

https://www.linkedin.com/in/jennifer-l-lovett-a2a3348/

Jeremy Cochran, President, Americas, Stein IAS

https://www.linkedin.com/in/jeremycochransteinia

Jeremy M. Evans, President of California Lawyers Association

https://www.linkedin.com/in/jeremymevansesq/

Jevon McCormick, CEO, Scribe Media

https://www.linkedin.com/in/jevonmccormick/

Jill Tomain, COO, Credit Union National Association

https://www.linkedin.com/in/jill-tomalin-42a122a/

Jim Leahy, CEO of USA Luge, Retired

https://www.linkedin.com/in/jim-leahy-82699a7/

Jim Strawn, President, Jim Strawn & Company

https://www.linkedin.com/in/jimstrawn/

Jim Traister, CEO of The Digital Navigator

Joan Quintana, Managing Director, AdventGX

https://www.linkedin.com/in/joanquintana/

John Felton, President/CEO of Riverstone Health

https://www.linkedin.com/company/riverstone-health

John Formica, Hotel Resort Leader, Walt Disney Company (retired), Motivational Speaker

https://www.linkedin.com/in/john-formica-the-ex-disney-guy/

John Naber, Owner at Naber & Associates

https://www.linkedin.com/in/john-naber-oly-754959/

John Norden, VP, Pricing at General Dynamics Information Technology

https://www.linkedin.com/in/john-norden-1aa651/

John Petrisko, Medical Director Employee Health, Billings Clinic

https://www.linkedin.com/in/john-petrisko-md-mph-cmro-73222111/

John Murray, Managing Director, Research Circle Technology, GE Healthcare (retired)

Jordan Goldmeier, Founder, The MoneyMaking Machine Newsletter

https://www.linkedin.com/in/jordangoldmeier

Jon Tester, US Senator, Montana

Jose Quintana, President, AdventGX, Founder of Innovation Underground
    https://www.linkedin.com/in/josequintana/
JP Pomnichowski, State Senator, MT
    https://www.linkedin.com/in/jp-pomnichowski-2642561/
Joseph Fluder, CEO/President, SWCA
    https://www.linkedin.com/in/joseph-fluder-36134628/
Judy Casperson, VP, Key Bank
    https://www.linkedin.com/in/judy-casperson-1baa095/
Judy Peppler, President and CEO, KnowledgeWorks Foundation (retired)
    https://www.linkedin.com/in/judy-peppler-94280759/
Julie Mosely, CEO of J Strategies
    https://www.linkedin.com/in/julie-mosley-23554a7b/
Karen Gilhooly, HSBC, Senior Executive Leader, Financial Services and Global Transaction Banking
    https://www.linkedin.com/in/karen-gilhooly-974611a3/
Kartik Shankar, SVP Engineering, Jefferies
    https://www.linkedin.com/in/kartikshankar/
Kathy Anchors-Budd, President/CEO, National Credit Union Management   https://www.linkedin.com/in/kathy-anchors-budd-0aaa684/
Kathy Chou, SVP of SaaS Engineering at Nutanix
    https://www.linkedin.com/in/kathychou1/
Kelly Coleman, Owner, and CEO of Hancock Enterprises and P3Coleman Properties
    https://www.linkedin.com/in/kelly-coleman-7010b117/
Ken Baris, CEO/Chief Visionary BHHS Jordan Baris Realty
    https://www.linkedin.com/in/kenbaris/
Kim Meier, Co-Owner, Meier Family Chiropractic
Kimberly Miner, Chairman/CEO Envision You Victory Over Violence Non-Profit Foundation
    https://www.linkedin.com/in/kimberly-miner-b4584015/
Krishna Bhakar, Founder/CEO of Ribon Gum Pvt. Ltd,
    https://www.linkedin.com/in/krishnabhakar/
Kyra Tehve Swallow, Chief of Staff, Banfield Pet Hospital
    https://www.linkedin.com/in/kyra-tehve-swallow-71842a83/

Laurie Lachance, President, Thomas College
https://www.linkedin.com/in/laurie-lachance-56552655/
Laurie Stewart, President/CEO of Sound Community Bank
https://www.linkedin.com/in/lauriescb/
Len Morrissey, Managing Partner at Morrissey, Metcalfe, and Associates LLC
https://www.linkedin.com/in/lenmorrissey/
Lenette Kosovich, CEO of Rimrock
https://www.linkedin.com/in/lenette-kosovich-442818b/
Leslie Ruyle, Executive Director of the Bush School of Government and Public Service/Research Scientist at Texas A & M University   https://www.linkedin.com/in/leslie-ruyle-3459b343/
Linda Patten, CEO, Dare2Lead With Linda
https://www.linkedin.com/in/lindapatten/
Lisa King, CEO, Magnifi U
https://www.linkedin.com/company/magnifi-u-inc/
Luis Lemaitre, Group VP, Oracle, North American Cloud
https://www.linkedin.com/in/luis-lemaitre-05879520/
Major General Jim Hoyer
https://www.linkedin.com/in/james-hoyer-2285a1143
Marc Ashworth, CIO, First Bank, Greater St. Louis
https://www.linkedin.com/in/marcashworth/
Marcus Peralta, SVP at Mastercard,
https://www.linkedin.com/in/pertau/
Marcella Gencarelli, VP, Manager of Client Engagement, Lakeland Bank   https://www.linkedin.com/in/marcellagencarelli/
Marco Sylvestre, Vice-President Product Development, Venzee Technologies, Inc.
https://www.linkedin.com/in/marcosylvestre/
Margaret O'Neal, CEO of United Way, WV
https://www.linkedin.com/in/margaret-oneal-4981a021/
Marie Olson, Executive Operation Director, Soundtransit
https://www.linkedin.com/in/marie-olson-845317196/
Mark Geiselmayor, VP, Sales and Business
https://www.linkedin.com/in/mark-geiselmayr/

Mark Vergenes, President, MIRUS Financial Partners
    https://www.linkedin.com/in/markavergenes/
Marty Roth, President, University of Charleston
    https://www.linkedin.com/in/martyrothphd/
Marv Hodges, Division Leader, PFS Investments
    https://www.linkedin.com/in/marv-hodges-9a59594/
Mary Ann Dunwell, Montana Senator
Mary Kay Bates, CEO at Bank Midwest
    https://www.linkedin.com/in/mary-kay-bates-b20a0ba/
Mary D. Madden, President/CEO Hudson Valley Credit Union
Maureen Niemiec, VP, IT, Internal Auditing, Flagstar Bank
    https://www.linkedin.com/in/maureenniemiec/
Max Baucus, U.S. Senator 1978-2014, longest-serving senator
from Montana
    https://www.linkedin.com/in/max-baucus-704180146/
Michael Frankel, SVP of Sales, North America at Selerant
    https://www.linkedin.com/in/michael-frankel-088870/
Michael George, CEO, Invicti
    https://www.linkedin.com/in/michaelgeorgeboston/
Michael Lewis, Area Manager, NurseCore
    https://www.linkedin.com/in/mrmichaelalewis/
Michael Rider, Project Manager, Avitus Group
Michael S. Segal, SVP, Merger Integration Manager II,
    https://www.linkedin.com/in/michaelssegal/
Michelle Boxx, CEO, Boxxbury
    https://www.linkedin.com/in/theblondefixer/
Michelle Foster, CEO/President, Greater Kanawha Valley
Foundation
    https://www.linkedin.com/in/michelle-foster-ph-d-
13701812/
Michele Redman, Head Women's Golf Coach, the University of
Minnesota (retired)
Mike King, CEO of Volunteers of America
    https://www.linkedin.com/in/mike-king-87490940/
Mitze Amorosco, SVP, CIO, Director of Information Services,
ArchCare
    https://www.linkedin.com/in/mitzeamoroso/
Nadya Rousseau, Founder, Alter New Media
    https://www.linkedin.com/in/nadyarousseau/

Nandini Srinivasan, VP, Quality Assurance at Motive
https://www.linkedin.com/in/nandini-srinivasan-9b3b39/
Neil Greer, CEO, and Co-Founder of Impact Engine
https://www.linkedin.com/in/neilgreer/
Norman Frederick, VP, SVP, Partner, NTT Data Services
https://www.linkedin.com/in/norman-f/
Norman Kromberg, Managing Director, NetSPI
https://www.linkedin.com/in/normankromberg/
Pam Farris, CEO of WV Leadership
https://www.linkedin.com/in/pam-farris-0552a09/
Patti Leichliter, CFO/COO, Three Rivers Bank of Montana
https://www.linkedin.com/in/patti-leichliter-8717b035/
Patrick Byrne, CEO, GE Renewable Energy Onshore Wind
https://www.linkedin.com/in/pat-byrne/
Paul Brady, SVP and CIO of the Arbella Insurance Group
https://www.linkedin.com/in/paul-brady-9100492/ \
Peter Adriaens, Professor and Entrepreneur, Co-Founder of
Equarius Risk Analytics
https://www.linkedin.com/in/peteradriaens/
Peter George, CEO, Evolv Technology
https://www.linkedin.com/in/peterggeorge/
Randie Lawson, CEO, Mountain State Waste Company
Rich Sheridan, CEO, Menlo Innovations
https://www.linkedin.com/in/menloprez/
Richard Lowe, President, and CEO of Franchise Services
https://www.linkedin.com/in/richlowe/
Richard Lowney, Co-Founder and CTO of MiEdge
https://www.linkedin.com/in/richard-lowney-141ab/
Richard Maack, VP, APG Polymer
Rich Sheridan, CEO, Chief Storyteller, Menlo Innovations
https://www.linkedin.com/in/menloprez/
Richard Serpa, VP, Mid-Market of Kyriba
https://www.linkedin.com/in/richardserpa/
Rodney Walker, President of Grant Central USA
https://www.linkedin.com/in/rodneywalker180/
Rosandra Silveria, SVP, Fortune 500
Ryan Gregory, CEO Wyoming Roofing
https://www.linkedin.com/in/ryan-g-15a60261/

Ryan Lauderdale, CEO, Rypen Fitness
https://www.linkedin.com/in/ryan-lauderdale-88773b43/
Sam Hocking, President/Co-Founder, Vertis,
https://www.linkedin.com/in/samhocking/
Samantha Howell, VP, HR, Hanes Companies, Inc.
https://www.linkedin.com/in/samantha-howell-80854816/
Samuel Seisdedos, VP and Head of Operations, Ericsson
https://www.linkedin.com/in/samuelseisdedos/
Sandra McDonough, President, and CEO of Oregon Business & Industry (retired)
https://www.linkedin.com/in/sandra-mcdonough-06aa9520/
Scott Coleman, COO of Fenice Community Media
https://www.linkedin.com/in/scottcoleman/
Sean O'Neill, Two-Time Olympian, Three-time USA Paralympian Coach
Seth Greene, CEO, Market Domination LLC
https://www.linkedin.com/in/sethgreene/
Shari Krikorian, Payment Executive, Digital Transformation and Product Development, MasterCard (retired)
https://www.linkedin.com/in/sharikrikorian/
Sheila Lamberson, Technology Manager, State Farm
https://www.linkedin.com/in/sheila-lamberson-cpcu-clu-chfc-pmp-crisc-a0183584/
Shireen Yates, CEO of NIMA (retired)
https://www.linkedin.com/in/shireentaleghani/
Souheil Badran, EVP, COO, Northwestern Mutual
https://www.linkedin.com/in/souheilbadran/
Steve Bottfeld, CEO of Marketing Solutions, retired
https://www.linkedin.com/in/steve-bottfeld-6a2211a/
Steve Corsi, CEO of Volunteers of America Western Washington (VOAWW),
https://www.linkedin.com/in/steve-corsi-24086757/
Steve Ross, VP, Sales Development, Outreach
https://www.linkedin.com/in/thesteveross/
Steve Torgeson, CTO, United Language Group
https://www.linkedin.com/in/stephentorgeson/

Steven Birdsall, EVP, Global Sales
    https://www.linkedin.com/in/birdsall/
Sunmeet Jolly, Founder/CEO, GROTU
    https://www.linkedin.com/in/sunmeet/
Surjya Misra, VP, Client Services, Virtusa
    https://www.linkedin.com/in/surjyamisra/
Susan Moffett, SVP, BCG Digital Ventures
Suzette Turnball, MBA, Ph.D., Program Manager, Higher
Education Administration, Educator
    https://www.linkedin.com/in/suzturnbull/
T.R. Ramachandran, CEO, AEye, Inc.
    https://www.linkedin.com/in/t-r-ramachandran-
23760a4/
Takehiko Nakamura, CEO of Blue United Corporation
    https://www.linkedin.com/in/tnakamura/
Terrence Mills, CEO, Founder, Director, Veuu Incorporated
    https://www.linkedin.com/in/terencemills/
Thomas Bouchette, President of Citizens Bank
    https://www.linkedin.com/in/thomas-bouchette-
7527a199/
Till Paris, CEO, Dream Team Media
    https://www.linkedin.com/in/tillparis/
Tim Patneadue, EVP, COO, HSA Bank
    https://www.linkedin.com/in/timpatneaude
Tim Stanley, President, Total Document Solutions
Timothy Alcorn, CEO of Alcorn Media
    https://www.linkedin.com/in/timothyalcorn/
Tina Lucas, SVP/Asset Based Lending Manager of WaFd Bank
    https://www.linkedin.com/in/tina-lucas-a2581b9/
Tuff Harris, CEO of One Hear Warrior
    https://www.linkedin.com/in/tuff-harris-76720165
Tye Taylor, CEO Sunrise Media
    https://www.linkedin.com/in/tye-n-taylor/
Wayne Nelson, President of Stockman Bank,
    https://www.linkedin.com/company/stockman-bank/
Wesley Eugene, CIO, IDEO
    https://www.linkedin.com/in/wes-eugene/

Zachary Jones, President, First Market Bank
    https://www.linkedin.com/in/zacharyjjonescoach/detail
s/experience/
Zaza Soriano, Interim CTO, TeleSMART Health, CEO, ZaaWink
    https://www.linkedin.com/in/shikgluon/